£28.50

Building a better team

Peter Moxon
of Peter Moxon Associates

Building a better team

A handbook for managers and facilitators

Gower

Published by
Gower Publishing
Gower House
Croft Road
Aldershot
Hampshire GU11 3HR
England

Gower
Old Post Road
Brookfield
Vermount 05036
USA

Reprinted 1994

British Library Cataloguing in Publication Data

Moxon, Peter
  Building a Better Team: Handbook for
  Managers and Facilitators
  I. Title
  658.4

    ISBN 0–566–07424–9

Library of Congress Cataloging-in-Publication Data

Moxon, Peter.
    Building a better team : a handbook for managers and facilitators
  / Peter Moxon.
      p.   cm.
    Includes index.
    ISBN 0–566–07424–9 : $49.95 (est.)
    1. Work groups—Handbooks, manuals, etc.   2. Strategic planning-
  -Handbooks, manuals, etc.   I. Title.
  HD66.M69   1993
  658.4′02—dc20   93–20443
                                                                 CIP

 Typeset in 11pt Times by Raven Typesetters, Ellesmere Port, S. Wirral
and Printed in Great Britain at the University Press, Cambridge

To my father

Contents

Illustrations

Figures

Tables

Foreword

It was Pierre de Coubertin who said 'The most important thing in the Olympic Games is not winning but taking part'. To be part of an effective winning team, whether on the sports field or in a business environment, should always be our goal. Team building has become a vital management skill and a prerequisite for good management. To build a better team is a challenge, for the dynamics of a team are highly complex and getting a team to work effectively takes time and effort.

Effective teams can lead to much greater creativity, improved job satisfaction and motivation, increased energy and excitement, faster and more effective implementation of ideas and better use of individual skills and abilities. Peter Moxon's handbook is designed to do just that as he seeks to link the theory and practice and explains the underlying concepts behind effective team building. The major focus, however, of this handbook is in providing useable tools and techniques and pragmatic advice based on Peter's wide and knowledgeable experience to enable the practitioner to build a better team.

Tony Taylor
Institute of Training and Development

Preface

The introduction of flatter management structures, the trend towards flexible working and the spread of such initiatives as Total Quality Management, Investors in People and BS5750 have all brought into relief the need for teambuilding and the effective functioning of teams at all levels within organizations.

The fears of individuals asked to participate in teambuilding programmes, however, can be very real, especially when you are dealing with 'live teams'. A badly implemented teambuilding session can have long-term detrimental effects on the working relationships within a team.

Much of the resistance to teambuilding is based on bad past experiences or preconceived notions that teambuilding is a threatening process involving 'baring of the soul' or personal attack from others. This should not be the case. A well thought through design, based on an initial diagnosis and facilitated skilfully, can produce satisfying results for all involved, allaying fears and actively encouraging participation.

How then do you develop such safe strategies, which on the one hand avoid glossing over issues which inhibit team performance, whilst on the other provide for an enjoyable and constructive process? This is the challenge that faces both the manager of the team and any internal facilitator or trainer involved in helping. It is that question that this book seeks to address.

The skills involved in the designing and running of effective teambuilding programmes are readily learnable and should no longer be regarded as the preserve of the external specialist. They are the same skills required by managers who seek to become coaches and enablers of their people, and to that end the book should be of equal interest to manager and internal facilitator alike.

The basic aim of the book is to present those learnable skills for use by others. It is intended to be a comprehensive, practical handbook for those who want to set up and run successful teambuilding programmes with working teams. Whilst time is taken to explain the concepts underpinning teambuilding the emphasis of the book is on providing usable tools and advice based on many years of personal experience. It offers not a universal formula for success but a palette of ideas and some simple frameworks that together can be used with a high degree of flexibility.

Every team is unique. Much of the enjoyment of working with them is in understanding and analysing each particular team's problems and developing solutions that have relevance and meaning to the individuals involved.

It is my hope that this book will play its part in removing the myths and fears surrounding teambuilding. For both the facilitator and manager teambuilding can be a challenging and enjoyable experience. There can be few things more satisfying for a manager than watching his or her group develop into an effective team whose results seem to flow effortlessly as a natural extension of the way they work together – but then I'm biased!

Peter Moxon

Acknowledgements

Without the direct support of some of my closest clients and friends it is true to say that what follows would never have become a first book. It seems only appropriate that their contributions should be acknowledged.

The stimulus and sponsorship to write the first draft came from Graham Vitty, Personnel Director of Glaxo Manufacturing Services. His continued prompting over several years eventually pushed me into writing this first publication. Much of the experience crystallized in the text was gained working alongside Graham and his colleagues in Glaxo over a long period.

My thanks also go to an old friend Elizabeth Burrows who worked hard to translate my handwriting into intelligible type-written text – an unenviable task.

Lastly my thanks must go to my wife Margaret and my son Daniel. Between them they have continuously and without complaint endured my lifestyle as a consultant, without which there would be little to write about. Over the last twelve months in particular they have put up with the late hours and absence of company, and helped critique both the content and style of my writing to help produce something that I hope will help fellow travellers.

PM

Introduction

For all managers today the leadership and development of teams is central to their ability to achieve results through other people – as if it has ever been any different! However some managers may wish to view it, teambuilding is not a bolt-on process they can choose to apply when they have time, but a necessary part of their role. It is a style of managing a workgroup in such a way that the group comes to recognize the need for more effective teamwork as a means of improving its overall results. Also, it is practical, action-centred and very much a part of being a successful manager.

At its simplest it can be an informal, open dialogue between the manager and his or her team, conducted in the workplace as part of a regular team meeting. At its most complex it can be a series of preplanned two- to three-day workshops held off-site, working through a number of structured exercises.

The process of developing a team, however, does require skill and needs to be handled sensitively. The ramifications of an ill-conceived or badly run programme can stay with a team for a long time, since the issues being addressed are often personal, deeply felt and very important to the individuals concerned.

How to use the book

The book is divided into three parts. Each part is conceived with a separate theme in mind but together they provide sufficient theory and practical advice to enable a manager, trainer or facilitator to

prepare for, design and conduct a teambuilding programme. Part I concentrates on concepts and definitions, whilst the other two parts focus on tools and techniques.

Experienced trainers and facilitators may prefer to skip Parts I and II and use Part III as a palette of ideas to pick from and include in their own programmes. The exercises can be used as they stand or with modification.

Less experienced individuals are advised to read Parts I and II before starting. The background given will help the reader develop an appropriate design and choose the best timing and sequencing for the exercises described in Part III. In this way the reader will gain most value from the activities in the book and avoid obvious pitfalls by matching their use with the readiness and level of the group's development.

Teams and teambuilding

Part I explains the difference between a group and a team and describes the typical issues and problems experienced by all teams. It is the hierarchy of issues outlined here that provides one element of the basic framework for designing effective, non-threatening programmes.

Part I goes on to explore how groups develop naturally and the processes by which the levels of trust and openness are increased within a group. The changing behaviours displayed as a group grows are covered so that the reader can assess the current stage of development of the group they are working with.

The final section presents an overview of what teambuilding is and is not, what a teambuilding programme looks like, and what it involves the manager and team in doing. There is also guidance as to when a manager is likely to need the help of a facilitator and some specific criteria to help the manager make his or her decision.

Designing and running teambuilding programmes

Part II takes the reader through a logical process for preparing for and running programmes. It includes a four-stage model and practical details to help the reader apply the model to their own situation.

The emphasis throughout is on 'how to'. Typical problems and difficulties found during both the design and running of workshops are included together with possible solutions. Advice is given on how to handle discussions and how to tackle the more predictable problems that can arise, such as hidden agendas, conflicts, dominant and quiet members etc.

Teambuilding tools and techniques

Part III provides a collection of activities that can be used by the reader within their own designs. The exercises include practical tools to diagnose the current effectiveness of a team, and to tackle team issues such as decision-making processes, effectiveness of meetings, goal clarity, introducing a new team member etc. Together they cover the range of issues that commonly arise when working with a group.

Each exercise has been designed as a stand-alone activity to be run either separately or in combination with other exercises during a longer programme. All of them have been used extensively with real teams. For each activity, specific objectives are given and advice on how each activity runs in practice; predictable outcomes are described, as are possible difficulties and how either to avoid or handle them. The exercises have also been chosen to illustrate the use of a variety of methods – questionnaires, syndicates, buzz groups etc. The handout material in this section has been designed to be photocopied at 125% onto A4 sheets.

Summary

All groups go through the same natural processes of growth – from the first cautious conversations as individuals try to find their own role within the group, to the easy comfort of an effective team whose results seem to come effortlessly and as a natural extension of the way they work. An effective teambuilding programme offers a quicker route through the various stages, some of which can be difficult and uncomfortable for the group.

It must be remembered, however, that every group is unique and there is no universal design which, if used, will miraculously produce the perfect team. Some groups never fully develop within their natural lifetime, but all groups can be helped to increase their effectiveness in some measure.

The success of any teambuilding programme and, in particular, whether it represents a constructive or a destructive process, depends largely on the skills of the facilitator or manager running the sessions. A carefully developed programme skilfully run can
accelerate the growth of any group towards improved results and at

the same time can provide an enjoyable learning process for all those participating.

It is hoped that what follows will give managers and facilitators involved in teambuilding both the confidence and the skills to succeed in their endeavours.

Part I—Teams and teambuilding

Introduction

To design and run effective teambuilding programmes both the facilitator and manager must have some appreciation of what differentiates a team from a group, how groups develop naturally and the typical problems and issues all groups face. Knowledge of how groups function and grow, combined with an understanding of the methods and techniques of teambuilding, will enable them to design and run effective teambuilding programmes.

Whilst this book is concerned primarily with teambuilding methods and techniques, attention is also given in Part I to group functioning and growth. This section is not intended to be a detailed study but it should give the reader a basic grasp of the subject, in addition to providing some simple models that can be used to help groups to understand what they are experiencing. The text relies upon some practical models that have been well researched by others in the field. More than once these simple concepts have helped me, personally, to make sense of what is happening within a group and decide what course of action to take.

1 | Teams and team effectiveness

What is a team?

What distinguishes a group of individuals from a team and what criteria would we use to describe an effective team? These are important questions to consider before embarking on 'teambuilding'.

A team is distinct from a group when it has the following attributes:

- A common purpose.
- Recognition by each individual as *belonging* to the same unit (i.e. team identity).
- Interdependent functions.
- Agreed norms or values which regulate behaviour.

Obvious statements perhaps, but worthy of further examination.

If you asked each individual in your team to write down what he or she thinks is the fundamental purpose of the team, you are unlikely to receive a set of identical answers. At best you may obtain a broad consensus, at worst a range of widely differing views. For example, two individuals from a senior management team responsible for a manufacturing unit may describe their team's purpose respectively as: 'to meet the suppliers' demands placed on us'; and 'to provide quality goods at a competitive cost'. You could argue that both views are equally valid. Nevertheless, the behaviour of those individuals will be dictated by their own personal opinions of the team's overall purpose. Thus it is easy to see why those two individuals, whilst members of the same team, could come into conflict when a decision needs to be made whether or not to ship product on time but with marginal quality. Many teams within organizations may have worked together for several years and yet may never have tested their individual assumptions about the team's purpose.

If we turn to the 'sense of belonging' and the 'interdependence' felt by individuals in teams we can again see potential sources of conflict or lack of collaboration. Both are easily identifiable features in a transient project team or a team focused tightly on, say, a production module. But flatter management structures and matrix-type organizations place individuals in teams of specialists where the sense of interdependence (i.e. the need for an individual to *have* to collaborate with another to do his or her basic job) is less strongly felt. A good example would be a management team over a business control unit which is made up of accounts, information technology (IT), purchasing and warehousing functions. The individual managers over each function, whilst placed in the same team organizationally, may see little need for close collaboration, viewing their tasks as highly independent.

Equally, leaner structures require fewer managers, which results in each manager being a member of several teams. In such situations it is easy for an individual to pick and choose which team he or she works hardest for – and it may not be your team!

And finally, 'agreed norms' – or, put more simply, a common code of practice with regard to things such as communication, decision making, handling conflict etc. Most teams operate with individuals spending 80 per cent of their time working on their own, the team only coming together for short periods either weekly or monthly. It is their agreed code of practice that provides the framework for each team member to operate without continual reference to other members when taking actions that affect the team. Without those agreed terms the potential for misinterpret-ation of action and resulting conflict or mistrust is high. The absence of such norms results in team meetings where dysfunctional behaviours are prevalent and even simple tasks seem hard to achieve.

A common purpose, team identity, interdependence and agreed norms form the foundation of an effective team. Agreed and accepted by all, they form the 'contract' which binds individuals to the team as willing participants. When teambuilding with a group you are consciously helping the group to examine these issues; helping them to clarify their primary purpose, establish team identitiy and agree acceptable ways of working.

5

How does a group develop?

Much research has been conducted into the processes that occur within groups. One set of conclusions reached is that, as it develops, a group will pass through a number of distinct, natural phases, as shown in Figure 1. Whilst a teambuilding approach will, in a structured way, help groups move more quickly through these stages, they cannot be bypassed if the outcome is to be a mature, healthy and productive team. The stages are predictable and to some extent controllable. They have been defined by B. W. Tuckman[1] as:

- Stage I: Forming
- Stage II: Storming
- Stage III: Norming
- Stage IV: Performing

Each stage is unique and is characterized by certain types of individual behaviour and different issues faced by the team and the

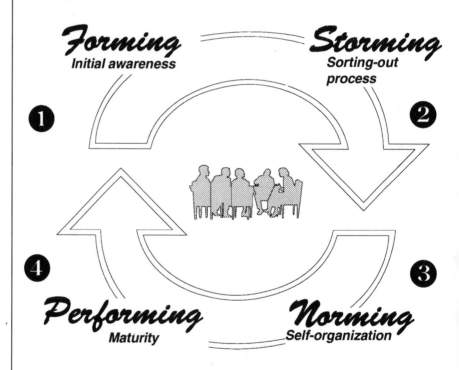

Adapted from B. W. Tuckman (1965), 'Development Sequence in Small Groups', *Psychological Bulletin*, 63, 284-499.

6 **Figure 1:** The four stages of group development

leader. As in the development and growth of an individual some stages may be more or less pleasant for the team to experience.

It sometimes happens that if the group is struggling during a particular stage they may start to fragment and want to give up the idea of working as an effective team. It is crucial, therefore, for the leader or facilitator to be able to recognize the symptoms and behaviours displayed during each stage. By understanding and recognizing a particular stage of the group's development he or she can help reassure the group (and him or herself if necessary!) that things are not going wrong, but that what they are experiencing and feeling is a natural part of their development.

Let us look at each stage – at the behaviour exhibited and the issues the group must face up to and work through.

Forming

Initial awareness – why we are here

As the name suggests this stage represents the group coming together initially. This would apply when the team is first formed or when new members come into the group.

Managers are constantly moving into and out of teams as they progress in their own individual careers. The make-up of teams therefore changes regularly. Indeed, one of the problems of senior management teams in particular is lack of stability, which prevents them having sufficient time together to mature fully. At the same time, at junior management and operator levels, individuals may have worked together for several years, yet the concept of team identity – as opposed to existing as a collection of individuals with the same boss – could be equally new. In this case the group needs to form or come together just as much as a newly appointed team.

During this stage people tend to be polite, with true feelings often withheld from fear of upsetting others or giving the wrong impression. Each individual in his or her own way will be trying to answer the question 'Will I be accepted'? Behaviour will be characterized by rules such as:

- keep ideas simple;
- say acceptable things;
- avoid controversy;
- avoid serious topics;
- if sharing feelings keep feedback to a minimum;
- avoid disclosure.

7

Cliques may start to form between kindred spirits or individuals who already know each other, although these are not generally destructive during this phase.

As well as individuals getting to know each other and settling in, the group as a whole is trying to establish why it is there and what its purpose is. This is especially so if the members of the team do not understand the need for its formation. For example, a fitter, an electrician and a planner are asked to report to a production team manager and become part of the operator team. For those three employees – who have probably worked alongside the operating team for several years, but reporting to separate functional managers – there could be great anxiety and even resistance to becoming a team member. In such a situation the group must take time collectively to reach consensus about its purpose and need to work as a team (although this may be done fairly superficially at first because members are still withholding their true views).

At the other extreme, if a project team is formed with a specific task, agreement on the team's purpose and objectives may be reached too quickly. They may decide to forgo discussion on the subject because they believe the answers are obvious. As they move into the next stage, however, they may find they have done this at some cost, since each member's interpretation of the obvious is subtly different. This can be a serious problem with highly task-focused teams or individuals who would regard talking about 'overall purpose' as a waste of time and simply want to get on with the job!

Finally, towards the end of this stage, the emergence of any cliques can begin to cause minor problems. Those not included in these cliques can begin to feel a little left out, or cliques may start to oppose each other (gently at first) as they try to influence the purpose and goals of the group towards their own needs.

During this first stage there is limited group identity and a strong dependence on the leader, as individuals each handle their own confusion, ambiguities and anxieties. They look to the leader to provide positive direction and remove uncertainty. According to the tolerance for ambiguity and the style and needs of its members, the forming stage of a group can be either smooth and pleasant or intense and frustrating.

Storming

Sorting-out process – bidding for control and power

This second stage represents the toughest stage for a group to work through and is marked by competition and conflict. Whilst potentially the most painful phase of the group's development it is probably the most important. During this stage the decision-making processes and mechanisms for control and influence are formulated – mechanisms critical to the effective functioning of the team.

During the forming stage people have become accustomed to being in the group and have developed some understanding of its purpose and goals. In doing so they will have suppressed some of their personal needs in order to be seen to collaborate. In this next phase members are starting to assert themselves – to regain their individuality, power and influence and to satisfy their need for respect from others. Examples of behaviour characteristics will be:

- strongly expressed views;
- challenging the ideas of others;
- poor listening;
- challenging leadership, authority and position;
- withdrawal by some team members;
- full expression of emotions;
- lack of collaboration and competing for control;
- a high level of reacting or defending.

Cliques, if already formed, may have a negative effect, as members use them to gain support for their ideas and as a base to influence and control others.

Conflict within the group rises to a higher level than at any other stage in the group's development. Typical attempts to resolve conflict will be by voting and compromise, and may even resort to use of third-party arbitration. All of these methods will only suppress rather than resolve these conflicts, which are likely to continue to re-emerge in other ways.

The behaviour range and participation levels within the group are at their widest. Some people, averse to conflict, withdraw and say little. Others use it as the opportunity to compete and dominate the group with their views.

Almost as a reaction to the group's dependency on the leader in the forming stage, his or her leadership may now be openly challenged or resented, much as a parent's help to a child is rejected once the child reaches adolescence.

The extent of open display of any conflict can vary, dependent upon the position of the team in the organization. On the one hand, the tendency is for operator teams and junior management teams to be visibly open and straightforward. On the other hand, in senior management teams the conflict will be more hidden, with the use of cliques to develop power and the working of hidden agendas more prevalent. This situation is less to do with a difference in personnel at the top and bottom of the organization and more to do with factors such as their communication skills, accepted norms of behaviour associated with position, or a perceived risk to job security.

There is little group identity during the storming phase and sometimes the concept of the team is rejected as an ineffective way to work ('I could do the job faster myself!'). Some members try to run away from the conflict by retreating into their own jobs, finding excuses to avoid team meetings and attempts at collaborative working. Output from the group is still achieved during this period, but, because it is often the result of compromise, it is generally of lower quality. Attempts at creative input from individuals are rejected as 'them trying to get their way'.

It would be easy for the group to give up at this stage and blame personality differences. Indeed, some groups never mature past this stage. However, until the group can break out of the frustrating maze of destructive behaviours that are typical of the storming phase and establish acceptable processes for decision making and control they cannot move on to the third stage. Any attempt to do so will result in failure and a return to the first and second stages until the power issues are properly resolved.

Norming

Self-organization

The transition to this third stage is indicated by a distinct shift in the attitudes of the group members – from one of competition to one of collaboration. It is during this phase that the sense of team identity starts to emerge and the cliques start to dissolve. Examples of behaviour characteristics will be:

- active listening;
- shared leadership;
- methodical, systematic ways of working;
- preparedness to change preconceived views;
- receptiveness to others' ideas;
- active participation by all;
- conflicts seen as mutual problems to be resolved as opposed win–lose battles;
- open exchange of ideas;
- self-disclosure.

The leader's role moves to one of guiding and facilitating. His or her relationship with the group moves from that of counterdependence in the storming stage to healthy interdependence. Also, creativity can be high. Group members become receptive to each other's ideas, resulting in improvement in the quality and speed of decision making.

In the storming stage members were establishing their roles in the team, marking out their 'turf'. Working outside their individual roles would have been seen by others as threatening. In the norming stage, roles become more fluid and the group more prepared to use each person's unique talents in ways that best achieve the task. Individuals will frequently take on tasks which lie outside their normally defined role. A greater degree of tolerance for the strengths and weaknesses of each member exists. Group members will more readily compensate for another's weakness by offering support and help.

It is at this stage that the group starts to realize the qualitative and quantitative benefits of working collaboratively as a team. High levels of trust start to develop as the group moves into its final stage of development.

Performing

Maturity and mutual acceptance

In this fourth stage, the members experience an intense level of loyalty to the group. From the outside it is seen as 'closed' and it can be difficult for a new member to be inroduced into the group – more so if he or she has strongly opposing values to those already developed by the group. In this case, the group will need to return to the earlier stages and work back through them together.

Behaviour patterns will include, for example:

- high flexibility of contribution;
- high creativity;
- openness and trust;
- shared leadership;
- strong relationships;
- feelings of warmth towards other members;
- easy acceptance of differences of view.

The group is less dependent on structure; team resources are truly pooled; and it is comfortable with individuality, which no longer represents a threat but a unique talent or contribution that can be used.

Feelings of achievement are high, with the group readily reviewing its successes and failures and seeking to improve. Usually the group achieves more than is expected or can be explained by the

11

apparent talents of the individual group members. At times, it may abandon working on the task altogether and take time out simply to 'socialize' and enjoy the company.

Progression through the stages

The reasons that prompt a group to move from one stage to another vary. During the forming stage, the stimulus to move from 'getting to know each other' to working on purpose and goals is usually provided, if not by the leader, by a group member's desire to progress and start actioning things. Then, as group members become more aware of each other, the frustrations and differences will start to come to light and that will force the group into the storming stage. Usually this takes more than one person to open up and state his or her feelings.

It can often be a problem when one person sees the issues that need to be addressed but cannot get the rest of the group to take the risk of moving away from the comfort of the first stage. The individuals will express any frustrations to their clique or even to a third party, but will not feel ready to be so open in full group sessions. The problem for the facilitator can be one of slowing one individual down, whilst working to help the rest of the group develop to the same state of readiness.

The main barrier between the storming and norming stages will be the unwillingness or inability of members to listen to and understand each other instead of reacting, jumping to conclusions, and then either attacking or defending. If a strong sub-group dominates in the storming stage, they can seriously hold back the whole group's development – as can a leader who is averse to conflict and diffuses it rather than allows it to be voiced and handled (which can also be a problem for a facilitator who dislikes emotional situations!).

Finally, the transition from the third to the fourth stage usually requires unanimous agreement by all members since there has to be a high level of mutual trust by all parties to operate at that level.

The process of moving a group through these stages of development cannot be forced – it is not something that is done *to* a group. The main reason for this is that each member must be prepared to give up something at each step in order to move forward. In particular:

– Moving from the first to the second stage requires letting go of comfortable discussion and starting to take real risks and share real feelings – possibly with resultant personal attacks by others.

Stages of development	Characteristic behaviours	Issues addressed		
		Task	*Interpersonal*	*Leadership*
Forming *Initial awareness – why are we here?*	- simple ideas - saying 'acceptable' things - avoiding controversy - avoiding serious topics - keeping feedback and shared feelings to a minimum - avoiding disclosure	- Introductions - Team purpose - Objectives	Inclusion *Will I be accepted?*	Dependence
Storming *Sorting-out process—bidding for control and power*	- strongly expressed views and poor listening - challenging leadership and authority - withdrawal by some - full expression of emotions - lack of collaboration and competing for control - reacting or defending	- Operating rules - Decision-making processes - Communication processes - Authority levels	Control *Will I be respected?*	Independence
Norming *Self-organization*	- shared leadership - methodical ways of working - preparedness to change preconceived views - receptiveness to ideas - active participation by all - mutual problem solving versus win—lose confrontation - open exchange of ideas	- Relationships - Interfaces	Affection *How can I help the group?*	Inter-dependence
Performing *Maturity and mutual acceptance*	- high flexibility of contribution - high creativity - openness and trust - shared leadership - strong relationships - feelings of warmth towards other individuals - easy acceptance of differences of view	- Productivity	Affection *How can we do better?*	Inter-dependence

Adapted from B. W. Tuckman (1965), 'Development Sequence in Small Groups', *Psychological Bulletin*, 63, 284-499.

Figure 2: The natural stages of group development

- Moving from the second to the third stage requires individuals to stop defending their own view and accept that they may be wrong or that others may have better ideas.
- Moving from the third to the fourth stage requires a high level of trust in others by the individual and placing him or herself in a vulnerable position with respect to them.

For these reasons, groups may proceed through all four stages quickly or slowly. They may be held up on any stage, or they may move quickly through one and slowly through others.

By moving on from a stage without properly resolving the issues involved, it is likely that the group will start to experience problems and need to go back. For example, a highly action-oriented group which does not spend sufficient time on the first stage can easily encounter problems in the second stage with sub-groups or individuals pursuing differing and conflicting objectives. Similarly, the introduction of a new member or leader will require a return to the first stage in order to bring the new people up to speed and allow them to 'buy in' to the tough decisions previously reached in the first and second stages. A good example of this would be the earlier case of the fitter asked to report to the production team manager.

If the group stays together long enough to reach the performing stage, it is possible for them to recycle through the whole process again, only this time working at a deeper level of discussion and debate and developing ultimately deeper trust and higher levels of effectiveness.

These then are the natural processes by which all groups develop – aided by the teambuilding process. The stages are summarized in Figure 2.

How are trust and openness developed?

As groups move through the cycle from forming to performing, two underlying traits develop strongly: the levels of openness within the group and the depth of trust between individuals. One of the goals of any teambuilding process must be to actively develop these two aspects of group behaviour. In a working environment the reason for this is not, as some people fear, to produce 'happy families'. First, it is to provide an easy climate in which conflicts and differences can be dealt with quickly, ensuring *all* the team's energies can be focused on the task. Second, it allows individuals to work effectively on their own, or in sub-groups, on issues that directly affect the whole team. The concept of a team doing everything together is neither productive nor healthy in the long term. However, without the right levels of trust and openness such activities provide a medium for suspicion and doubt about the motives behind others' actions.

In the early stages of group development when trust levels are low and views withheld it is difficult, if not impossible, for single members or sub-groups to take decisions on behalf of the whole group. At best they will only be allowed to do the ground work and make a recommendation. Equally, all team members will want to be party to important decisions to ensure that their own interests are fully catered for. This process can be both time-consuming and frustrating for a group.

In contrast, when appropriate levels of trust and openness have been developed, members are more prepared to lessen their involvement in decision making. They now have confidence that those taking specific decisions or actions will appreciate and look after all the group's interests. If it is seen that this does not happen, then benefit of the doubt will be given, concerns will be quickly shared and the potential for conflict diffused. Clearly, this climate within the group allows for a much more effective use of time and resources.

The Johari Window

The mechanisms for developing high levels of trust and openness are best described using a model called the Johari Window developed by J. Luft and H. Ingram.[2] The model (see Figure 3) describes how effective working relationships are developed through the processes of self-disclosure and feedback. It uses the analogy of a window with four panes. If we consider a relationship between two people, we can look at it in terms of what each person knows about the other (i.e. what is open) and what they do not know (i.e. what is hidden). In the model this is shown by two dimensions: information known and unknown to self; and information known and unknown to the other. The four resulting window panes represent four areas of effectiveness in the relationship.

Arena

The 'arena' is the area in which there is mutual understanding and shared knowledge. In other words, the information in that area is known to both the individuals. What is important is not the *quantity* of information that is known to both but the *quality*, that is, information *relevant* to them working together.

For example, it may be helpful for two people to know that they share a common interest in a particular sport – it will give them a point of conversation when they meet, but that is all. On the other hand, if a manager likes to be kept well informed and does not like surprises, it is essential for the personnel in his or her team to understand this requirement. Equally, if one of the team members is particularly independent and finds regular communication a chore, it helps the manager to know that. In both cases, without this shared knowledge, the potential for conflict can be readily seen. When each is aware of the other's needs, however, both parties can more easily tolerate their differences and understand why sometimes they may cause each other problems.

In a working relationship within a team, then, the more each person understands the needs, preferences and perspectives of others, the more effectively they can all work together. They do not have to agree with each other but they do need to understand why each will behave in particular ways.

Façade

It may be within this relationship between the two people that one decides *not* to share certain information. This may be for a variety of reasons, such as: mistrust of how the other person will react or use it;

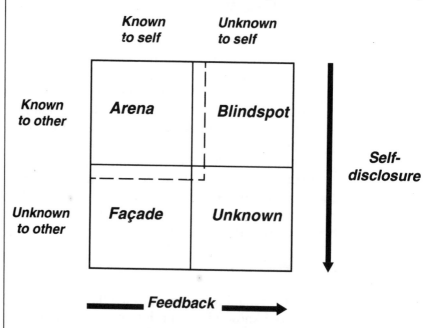

Adapted from J. Luft (1961), 'The Johari Window', *Human Relations Training News*, 5, 6–7; *Of Human Interaction*, Palo Alto, Calif: National Press Books.

| **Figure 3:** The Johari Window

a belief that it is private and of no relevance to work; or possibly fear of ridicule. That individual is then operating in the area of the 'façade'.

In itself, this may not represent a problem to the working relationship, unless the information is of consequence to the way these two people work together. For example, a group member may struggle with figures but not want to say so for fear of ridicule. If that person is asked by the manager to do a piece of work requiring heavy use of figures and the manager does not know of the problem, he or she may well start to get annoyed by an endless list of reasons put forward for delay in producing the work. Knowing of his colleague's difficulty will allow the manager to make choices, such as reassigning the work, helping the person involved or allowing more time.

In other words, the potential for misunderstanding and reduced effectiveness is there as long as the information is held in the 'façade'. This could represent a serious problem if the information relates to one person's basic respect for another's technical competence.

Blindspot

The same will apply to information in the 'blindspot', which represents the reverse situation to the 'façade'. Here information about the individual is known to the other person and not to the individual.

An example would be of two people, the first of whom is very talkative and does not listen. This greatly irritates the second person who as a result also proceeds not to listen every time the first person speaks. Clearly this is an unhealthy situation in a team environment. Why, you might ask, is the first person not aware of his or her behaviour and its impact on others? There could be two reasons. The first is an obvious one: no one has told him or her, or they have in the past and the feedback has been ignored. The second possible reason is that the person is simply not aware of his or her own behaviours and their possible impact. Until that information is moved from the person's 'blindspot' to his or her 'arena', there will always be a problem in the way the two people work together.

Unknown

The last area is the 'unknown'. Here, neither person is consciously aware of the information.

An example would be two people who regularly react badly to

each other but cannot understand why. Consider this situation. Two people, A and B, are talking together. B keeps interrupting A in mid-sentence, wrongly interpreting what A is trying to say. This means that A has to say 'No, that's not what I meant. What I meant was . . .' and re-explain the point. If this pattern of behaviour is repeated throughout the conversation A may start to feel very frustrated and annoyed but not know why. At the same time, B may be oblivious to what he or she is doing to annoy the other person. Until the two people both understand what is happening and how to avoid the destructive cycle, the situation cannot improve. In other words, the information stays hidden to both.

The four panes which together define a 'window' on the relationship are, then, the 'arena', the 'façade', the 'blindspot' and the 'unknown'. What the model is telling us is that the more quality information that is shared and understood between individuals, the more effective is likely to be the relationship. The larger the arena the more open the relationship will be, with less opportunity for misunderstanding and conflict.

In a working relationship, this does not necessarily mean big arenas are good and small are bad. The arena needs to be of an appropriate size depending on the extent to which the individuals need to work together. For example, a fitter and an operator working together daily in a packing team will need a larger arena than a systems designer and the end user who come together occasionally on projects.

How can individuals increase the size of their arenas? The mechanism involves two processes, called self-disclosure and feedback;

Self-disclosure   Self-disclosure is the sharing of important facts and feelings by the persons concerned. It involves taking risks by sharing views and giving feedback to others that may well cause a reaction in other people. At the same time, opening up with his or her own, deeper feelings makes that person vulnerable to breaches in trust or recrimination by others. For example, telling an autocratic boss he is inhibiting your ability to do your job effectively is never easy!

Feedback   Receiving feedback means not only actively seeking it, but also, most importantly, listening to it and acting on it. If a person is repeatedly given feedback and takes no action, the other person giving the feedback will eventually give up and a permanent block to effectiveness will exist.

What is important is that *both* processes are taking place to an equal extent. If not, a large blindspot or façade is developed. This is

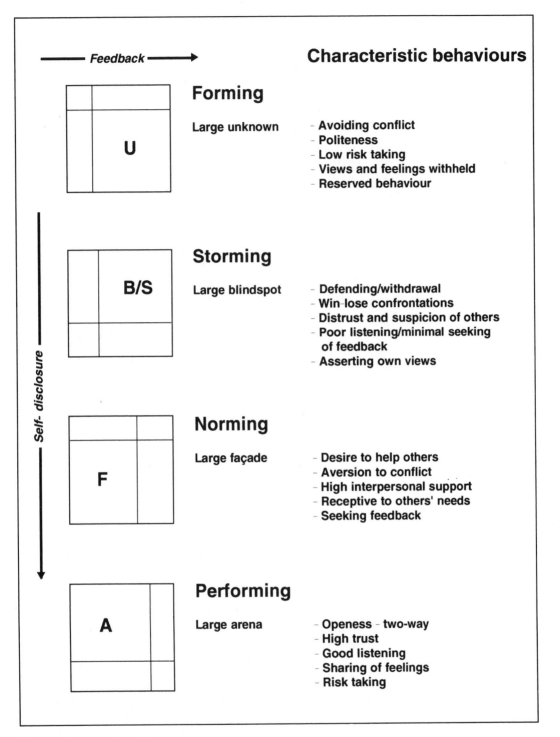

Figure 4: Johari profiles as team develops

demonstrated by the profiles shown in Figure 4. As the amount of self-disclosure and feedback increases the vertical and horizontal axis on the model are moved to the right or downwards respectively, producing differing 'profiles'.

If there is an excessive amount of self-disclosure compared to seeking feedback, the blindspot becomes the largest pane in the window. If the reverse is true the façade becomes the dominant pane. Both situations are unhelpful to the relationship.

When both sorts of behaviour are engaged in equally, the arena size increases and the unknown area reduces. As this process occurs neither the façade nor the blindspot increase in relative size with the associated problems that it may bring.

As the relationship between individuals and the group as a whole develops, the twin processes expand the arena, generating increasing levels of trust and openness, to a point where the size of the arena is appropriate to ensure effective working of the group. The group itself will judge when the levels of openness are sufficiently healthy.

The speed with which a group can open out the arena will vary because it does involve risk taking by individuals. For some, being very open comes naturally, for others it represents a threatening process. One of the dangers is that if some members of the group attempt to be too open too soon, it may drive reticent group members further into their shell.

The teambuilding process involves helping groups develop the skills of sharing feedback and self-disclosure, but in a way that minimizes the perceived risks to *all* team members. In reality, the risks are more imaginary than real. Nevertheless clumsy teambuilding processes, which try to force people to open up or receive feedback before they are ready, can do real damage. The skilful teambuilder helps the group open up the arena at a pace and to an extent that the group feels comfortable with. As noted earlier, some groups never develop the levels of openness needed to advance to the performing stage.

As the levels of openness increase, so should the depth of trust within the group. By being open, a person is potentially making him or herself vulnerable and giving the other person the power to 'harm' them. If that power is never abused, the trust becomes binding – the more power that is given, the deeper the trust will be. If it is abused, however, the reverse is true – the trust is lessened. In a trusting relationship there is room for mistakes and forgiveness when someone betrays a trust unknowingly. This would be the case in a group at the norming and performing stages. At the storming stage, however, this trust is not likely to be present since there is still real fear of the consequences of making oneself vulnerable to others.

To summarize, therefore, the Johari Window, in a different way, describes the processes by which groups develop. As they open up the arena they pass through the forming, storming, norming and performing stages, using the twin processes of self-disclosure and feedback. This is illustrated in Figure 4 where the different stages are represented by different 'windows'. Note how the 'storming' and 'norming' stages are characterized by unbalanced amounts of self-disclosure or feedback.

The model does point to a number of important conclusions which have an impact on the structuring and running of team-building sessions, as follows:

- Effective working relationships depend on shared knowledge and mutual understanding.
- The aim is to optimize the size of the 'arena' to that needed for the group to function effectively.
- Shared information needs to be relevant (i.e. quality versus quantity).
- Disclosure must involve both facts and feelings – the latter being more powerful but carrying higher risk.
- The level and depth of disclosure must be appropriate to the current stage the relationship has reached (i.e. not too much, too soon).
- Feedback needs to be sought, accepted, and acted upon. Also, acceptance of another's view does not necessarily mean 'agreed with'.
- An equal balance of feedback and self-disclosure is needed to prevent development of a large 'façade' or 'blindspot'.
- Different profiles exist for each relationship.
- Increasing the 'arena' size is a *joint* process involving risk taking by all parties.
- Opening out the 'arena' must not be unduly forced but can be encouraged.

What are the main problems encountered by teams?

The preceding sections were intended to clarify the phases that a group goes through as it develops and the processes it must use to create the levels of openness and trust which are prerequisites to high performance. Let us look now at the particular categories of problems experienced as the group moves through the phases, which will provide a practical framework within which help can be given through teambuilding programmes.

Team problems can be divided into four categories, as defined by Irwin, Plovnick and Fry.[3] These problems are common to all working teams, whether they are transient project teams or ongoing operational teams. The four categories are interdependent and form a natural hierarchy of issues as follows:

- Problems with *goals*
- Problems with *roles*
- Problems with *processes*
- Problems with *relationships*.

Problems with goals

A number of issues can occur with regard to the goals or objectives of the team. These can be summarized as follows:

- The extent to which the goals are clear and understood by all team members and are specific and measurable.
- The extent to which the goals are independent or interdependent; identifying whether they encourage joint or individual working.
- The extent to which the goals are owned and agreed by all team members and the extent to which they were involved in their development.
- The extent to which objectives have been shared within the team and the extent to which they create duplication or possible conflicts.

As was seen in the forming/storming model earlier, it is critical for the team's development that time is taken to establish clear goals to which all team members are committed. Initially this can be a trying experience, particularly with teams still at an early stage of development when members will challenge and argue vigorously over priorities and how achievable the objectives are. It is also surprising, in ongoing teams, how often members have not taken time to share their objectives with their colleagues in order to help others gain an understanding of their personal situation and pressures.

Problems with roles

It is only when a common view of the goals of the team is established that individual roles can be clarified. Put simply, if you do not know what game you are playing, how do you know what position to play? The types of issues that arise relating to roles are as follows:

- The extent to which each member understands the boundaries of his or her role and their degrees of freedom and authority.
- The extent to which an individual's view of their role matches what others in the team expect of them ('I thought *you* were doing that . . .').
- The extent to which possible overlap in responsibilities may cause confusion or conflict ('That's my job!', 'I thought you were supposed to be responsible . . .').

In existing teams, perceptions of each others' roles may vary widely. When a new member or leader joins a team, both they and the existing team members will have some firm, but probably differing, expectations of their new role. These expectations are never written down in job descriptions but they inevitably colour the judgements team members make about each other. Early and ongoing sharing of these expectations can prevent many issues from ever arising, and can remove opportunities for disappointment based on any misplaced expectation.

Problems with processes

In this category there are three broad areas.

Decision making

- Clarity of responsibility for decision making.
- Levels of authority and rights of veto.
- Who needs to be consulted before decisions are made.
- The extent to which decisions need to be made by consensus.
- How decisions are made in the absence of any individual.
- The ways in which decisions are communicated.

Communication and meeting processes

- What needs to be communicated to whom and by when.
- Balancing provision of information with overloading people with data.
- Individual tolerances for being kept informed and to what extent.
- The structure, content and frequency of various team meetings.

- Attendance at team meetings.
- The disciplines of meeting processes (e.g. time keeping, preparation, keeping on track etc.).

The team meeting represents an ideal opportunity to observe the effectiveness of the team. It is the focal point for the team coming and working together. Whatever issues are inhibiting team performance, they are likely to be cameoed and highlighted within any meetings, and they therefore provide the facilitator with a good opportunity to observe and understand the group's current stage of development.

For example, the meeting processes of a group in the storming stage will be in marked contrast to a group which has developed to the performing stage. In the former stage, typical issues will be poor time keeping, poor listening, and decisions made through voting. In the latter, there will be active listening, high collaboration, quick and easy decision making, and a regular review of process.

Leadership style

The leader's style and approach will have a marked effect on the processes and procedures adopted by the team when it is working together. The way he or she chooses to operate and behave can create as many issues as he or she may be trying to eliminate.

The nature of the leader's position of authority makes him or her a unique team member; and it is not simply a case of autocrats making poor team leaders and participative managers good team leaders. Moreover, as the group develops, the requirements placed on the leader will vary, as they will with the needs of each individual member.

One point is clear, however: for the team to develop and for a climate of openness and trust to exist, the leader must be prepared to seek and accept feedback both on his style and on the impact it is having on the group.

Problems with relationships

The final collection of issues relates to how the individuals within the team feel about each other, as follows:

- The extent to which they have respect for each other.
- The extent to which they understand and respect the needs of each other as individuals.
- The extent to which the basic values and attitudes of team members fit together or conflict.

Problems with goals

- Do people understand and accept the team's primary task?
- What are the team's priority objectives? Do all agree?
- How are conflicts in priorities handled?

Problems with roles

- What do team members expect of each other?
- Have these expectations been shared? Do they match?
- Do individual objectives fit with the team's overall objectives?
- Are there areas of overlap or duplication between team roles that could produce conflict?

Problems with processes

- How are decisions taken? Are authority levels clear?
- Are communication processes across the team working?
- Are structures, content and processes in meetings effective?
- How are problems and conflicts resolved?
- How is activity coordinated? Are reporting procedures understood and adhered to?

Problems with relationships

- How do team members treat and feel about each other?
- Are people's individual needs recognized and respected?
- Does the team climate allow for open debate and sharing of concerns?
- Do the team and leader encourage feedback on team and individual performance?

Adapted from I. M. Irwin, M. S. Plovnick, and R. C. Fry (1974), *Task-Oriented Team Development*, New York: McGraw-Hill.

Figure 5: Hierarchy of team issues

Such issues tend to be more deep seated and harder to resolve, especially in more senior teams within organizations. They can, however, be powerful determinants in the behaviour of team members towards each other. For example, the finance director who will not even look at the production director when he is addressed by him because he regards him as technically incompetent and not worth listening to! Relationship issues do not always emerge easily in working teams. If they are a serious inhibitor they will need to be resolved before the group can be fully effective. The solutions, however, may not come through a teambuilding programme but may require separate action by the leader with the members concerned. Thus, when pursuing a teambuilding programme with an existing team a judgement has to be taken by the leader as to how far he or she wishes to open up such issues within group sessions. In some cases it may be the leader's own reluctance to address the issue that prevents further group development.

Whilst relationship issues may impose a serious limitation on the potential growth of the group, it could be more tolerable to live with the problem, given the natural life cycle of the team. In that way the problem will resolve itself over time. It is important, however, that supposed personality clashes are not used as an excuse for failing to address underlying problems to do with goals, roles etc. Quite commonly, on closer examination, it will be found that a so-called personality clash is due to a lack of clarity of roles or to misplaced expectations with regard to decision making and responsibility. Furthermore, by working through the hierarchy of issues in the order given at the start, it is often the case that by the time the team has resolved issues to do with goals, roles and processes, the so-called personality clash will have evaporated.

To summarize, the goals–roles–processes–relationships model provides an ideal framework within which teambuilding programmes can be developed. By mirroring the hierarchy within the structure of your sessions it is possible to develop highly effective programmes that address the primary causes of problems whilst at the same time representing a non-threatening approach to individuals within the team. As you progress down the hierarchy, the issues discussed become more personal in nature. At the same time the levels of trust and openness will be growing, as will the preparedness of members to share deeper thoughts and feelings.

The model also provides the manager and facilitator with a ready checklist against which to analyse team issues and establish any need for teambuilding activity. A fuller description of methods for diagnosing current team effectiveness is covered in Part III, but the list of questions in Figure 5 should provide a good initial prompt.

References

1. Tuckman, B. W. (1965), 'Development Sequence in Small Groups'. *Psychological Bulletin*, 63, 284–499.

    Harvey, D. F., and Brown, D. R. (1988), *An Experiential Approach to Organisation Development*, 3rd edn, London: Prentice-Hall International, 223–5, 234–9.

    Hanson, P. C. (1973), 'The Johari Window: a model for soliciting and giving feedback', in *The 1973 Annual Handbook for Group Facilitators*, ed. Jones, J. W. and Pfeiffer, J. F., San Diego, Calif.: University Associates, 114–19.

2. Luft, J. (1961), 'The Johari Window', *Human Relations Training News*, 5, 6–7; *Of Human Interaction*, Palo Alto, Calif.: National Press Books.

3. Irwin, I. M., Plovnick, M. S. and Fry, R. C. (1974), *Task-Oriented Team Development*, New York: McGraw-Hill.

2 | Teambuilding

Definitions

Having briefly explored the natural processes by which groups grow and the issues they must confront, let us now look at how you can develop them through the structured approach offered by teambuilding.

Much has been presented and written about teambuilding – sufficient for it to be too often regarded as a separate management initiative or even as a potentially threatening experience. It is neither of these. All organizations are made up of groups of individuals who *have* to work interdependently. For any organization to be successful, those groups must operate as effective teams. And for any manager, with responsibility over others, to succeed, he or she must be able to lead and manage their team effectively. Teambuilding, therefore, is not a discretionary activity; it is and always has been an integral part of managing. Handled properly, teambuilding does not have to be a threatening exercise in which individuals feel that they will be expected to bare their innermost souls or face personal attack.

The aim of teambuilding is simply stated:

To help people who work together to function more effectively in teams and to assist the team itself to work more effectively as a whole.

The important words in this definition are 'effectively' and 'work' – teambuilding is not designed to build happy families or deep, meaningful relationships!

Effective teambuilding is concerned with the following functions:

- Improving performance and results.
- Making greater use of both individual and team strengths –not simply concentrating on weaknesses.
- Resolving problems about which something can and must be done, and which are within the responsibilities of the particular team involved.

In a working environment, the focus of any teambuilding programme has to be on improving performance and results, for this represents the primary purpose for that team's existence. As we have seen, the main difficulties affecting a team's performance are: problems with goals; problems with roles; problems with processes; and problems with relationships. These areas represent a *descending hierarchy* of issues which can provide a framework for team development. Only after the problems at each level are resolved, can the team productively address the next level down.

Too often, the blame for poor teamwork is laid on poor relationships between team members. These so-called personality clashes could be rooted in unclear objectives, conflicting responsibilities or differing perceptions of authority levels – in other words, problems to do with 'goals', 'roles' or 'processes', and little to do with 'relationships' in their purest sense. However, where the problems are due to fundamental relationship issues, asking individuals to talk about these problems to start with could be seen as risky and threatening, while starting by talking about the objectives of the team is not.

A safe strategy for pursuing teambuilding, therefore, is to help the team work through the issues in the order of the hierarchy. This will also allow time for the natural process to occur whereby a group develops trust and openness. As a group progresses down the hierarchy, the type of issue discussed becomes more personally focused, but, at the same time, the levels of group openness and trust increase. In this way, the perceived risk to individuals of sharing their deeper thoughts and feelings is lessened.

A second source of fear and concern regarding teambuilding is the exposure of weaknesses and feelings of being 'found out'. The impact of this problem can be lessened by not overconcentrating on these factors and by balancing any discussion of them with feedback on strengths. In many cases, the cause of a weakness can be a person overplaying a strength without being aware of it. For example, a person who is overly enthusiastic and a strong verbal presenter may be a poor listener and dominate a discussion unknowingly.

29 Finally, the team should concentrate its time on issues that it can resolve within its given areas of responsibility. It is easy to allow team sessions to degenerate into apportioning blame to those not present.

In conclusion, teambuilding in the workplace is a task-oriented activity. The task alone provides the context in which it becomes appropriate to discuss processes, procedures and individual behaviour. By following a structured approach that does not start directly with personal issues, teambuilding can be pursued in a non-threatening way.

What does teambuilding involve?

A typical teambuilding programme will include the following features, as outlined in Figure 6 (see p. 31).

Regular, possibly frequent, working sessions Teambuilding is an ongoing process with existing and new teams. In much the same way as a car needs regular servicing to make sure it runs well, so does a team. With a new team, there will be a need for an initial session for the team to agree its purpose, roles and a basic *modus operandi*. It will then need further sessions, possibly after a month or two, as members settle in and issues start to surface. With an existing team, ongoing sessions will be needed to create the environment in which any long-held, but hidden, frustrations and differences can be brought up and discussed. Even with a healthy, productive team, if no time is take to review processes, revisit objectives etc., its effectiveness will slowly decay. Team reviews for effective teams are simply a part of the way they operate.

The team tackling its own problems – possibly with third-party help Team sessions are not training workshops. They are problem-solving sessions, concentrating on work-related issues. Third-party help can provide a loose structure for the sessions and facilitate the discussion, helping the group to clarify and resolve issues for themselves.

An emphasis on identifying the root causes and on tackling real issues During problem-solving sessions, the team needs to get beyond symptoms to the underlying causes so that problems are permanently solved. Team members do not, however, concentrate solely on their weaknesses. They spend time looking at strengths and successes in order that they can learn and repeat what they do well; and they tackle real work-related issues and look for practical, workable solutions.

Openness and honesty displayed by individuals and a preparedness to take risks In the early stages of team development, discussions will be polite and, at times, superficial. As the team develops, the levels of openness rise and the numbers of hidden agenda items reduce. This requires risk taking by members as they share deeper feelings and give more honest feedback to each other.

Action orientation and commitment by all individuals to decisions reached Healthy team development is more than sharing views and, in the process, relieving tensions. People are prepared to commit themselves to actions and to bring about changes in the teams and their own ways of working. Each session will produce action plans which are followed up on the job and periodically reviewed.

Individual willingness to put in the time and effort Team development does require time away from the job on a regular basis. In the early stages, this can be sessions of two to three days followed up by a day a month for several months. Once the team is performing well, a day every six months may be enough, with regular process reviews of up to an hour being conducted monthly as part of their normal

- **Regular working sessions**

- **Tackling own problems - with help?**

- **Tackling root causes**

- **Openness, honesty and risk taking**

- **Action-orientation-commitment to decisions**

- **Individuals put in time and effort**

- **Leader accepts feedback**

- **Development of interpersonal skills**

- **Programme unique to team**

31 | **Figure 6:** Teambuilding programme characteristics meetings. For a transient team, such as a task force set up to work on some aspects of a new building, the time needed can be considerably less.

The leader prepared to accept feedback   For team development to work the leader's style and values need to be consistent with devolved decision making and consultation as a way of working. As with all the members of the team, he or she must be willing to accept feedback on personal behaviours that may be affecting team performance.

The development of interpersonal skills at some stage   Team development will highlight some skill deficiencies such as running effective meetings, listening, giving feedback etc. Team development programmes will often include some training sessions aimed at increasing skills. Effective teams not only work together but train together.

Each programme unique to a particular team   This aspect sets teambuilding apart from generic training where groups are put through identically structured programmes. All teams need to work through the same issues, but the programme depends on the starting point of the individuals and the team and any problems they have in working together effectively. The more skills-oriented the session, the more generic will be the input, and the role of the 'helper' shifts from facilitating towards training. With a very nervous group, training can provide an ideal way of creating opportunities for increasing openness and feedback.

Is a facilitator necessary?

The simple answer to this question is 'No'. In a healthy team, open discussion is the norm, there is respect for the leader and he or she actively consults with individuals. These circumstances allow constructive debate on the performance of the team without any third-party help. All that is needed is some structure for the sessions. This is not always the case, however, and it can be helpful to use a third party to initiate discussion and/or help develop the team until it is robust enough to cope unaided.

These are the following factors to consider in making the decision to use help, be it from an external or internal facilitator:

- The existing climate within the team and its current stage of development.
- The extent to which the leader's style contributes to any problems.

- The team's past experience with regard to teambuilding.
- The nature and seniority of the individuals within the team.
- The depth of feeling and nature of the issues present.

If we consider each factor in turn, the need to use help or not in any given situation will become clearer.

The existing climate

As a group moves through the natural stages of development – 'forming', 'storming', 'norming' and 'performing' – the climate of openness changes. In the first stage, the group is polite and members are guarded in their responses. In the second stage, opinions can be candidly, and often unskilfully, stated, with potential damage to others' feelings. The third and fourth stages, however, are marked by a shift in attitude towards collaboration, openness and a desire to help each other. The leader of the team should be able to handle these latter stages without help – or at least with help in the design and structuring of sessions only.

The situation is different in the first and second stages. The leader may feel the need for help to get the group to open up in the first stage, and to handle any open conflict or hidden agendas in the second stage. Help would be essential if there were also problems with the leader or if the team contained particularly forceful individuals.

In addition, during these early stages, members may be prepared to share concerns or issues with a neutral facilitator on a one to one basis, whilst still not feeling comfortable doing so in the group sessions. A skilful facilitator will use this confidential data in designing the group sessions in such a way that those same members will feel more comfortable sharing their views with the group, and he or she may also use the data to avoid individuals being put in too difficult a situation too soon.

For a leader to elicit such concerns from the team would require him or her to have a strong working relationship with each team member.

The leader's style

The personal style and approach of the leader is a crucial factor in deciding whether to seek help or not. For a teambuilding programme to work at all, the leader's behaviour must be consistent with shared decision making and consultation. He or she must feel comfortable spending time on the process (i.e. *how* the team operates) as much as on the task (i.e. *what* the team needs to achieve), and must be prepared to seek and accept feedback and then act on it.

If the leader's preferred style is inappropriate, it is likely that the working relationship will not be robust enough for team development to take place without help. The risks to team members – as perceived by them – may be too great to allow open, honest discussion. Moreover, it must be borne in mind that whilst the leader may feel that he or she has an open relationship, it is how that relationship is seen by the team members that counts. When the leader's behaviour is inconsistent and the working relationship not as strong as it needs to be, a third-party facilitator is in the best position to work with both parties to build the right climate for teambuilding to progress. Also, it is probable that in these circumstances the leader will initially be more receptive to neutral but honest feedback from a skilled facilitator than to feedback from a frustrated subordinate.

The team's past experience

The group's past experience of teambuilding, or the previous experiences of members within it, will have a bearing on how receptive the group will be to the leader's intentions. Past experiences, if good, can be a positive motivator for the group and allow the manager to progress without help. Bad experiences, however, last a long time in people's memories. Such experiences may have been with consultants, a particular leader or with types of teambuilding such as outdoor or sensitivity training that focus heavily on personal behaviours.

The individuals involved

The extent to which this factor is important is unique to each team. Strong, dominant members may be more easily handled by a facilitator than by the manager, who may be misread if he or she has to deal with such an individual in an open session. Skilled facilitators will be able to control aggressive individuals and, much as with a dominant leader, such a person may take personal feedback better from a facilitator.

The seniority of the team, or the trust levels between groups if an inter-group session is being run, may also require the manager to use help. For example, in a joint management and trade union workshop, the trade union representative may not feel comfortable without a neutral external facilitator. With a senior executive team, the underlying politics and perceived risk of being open may not allow a meaningful session to be run by the managing director alone.

The nature of the issues involved

This is a fairly obvious factor to consider. If the issues are deep seated (e.g. basic disrespect between individuals) or are of a long-standing nature, the use of a neutral facilitator may be essential.

These five factors should therefore be considered when making a balanced judgement on whether to use the help of a facilitator.

In order to operate effectively with the team the facilitator, especially if an internal trainer or consultant, must have personal credibility with the members. He or she should not be forced on a team, except perhaps on an initial trial basis.

One thing is clear, however, and that is the difference between the roles of the facilitator and the manager. The teambuilding programme *must* be seen as belonging to the manager. The facilitator's role is to provide a helping resource to start the process. Solutions and outcomes must be the manager's and the team's. The longer-term aim of the facilitator should always be to help the group develop the right levels of openness and skills to carry out teambuilding unaided as an ongoing part of their working together.

Summary of Part I

Teams have some distinct characteristics that mark them apart from a group of individuals that simply report through to a nominated manager on an organization chart. All groups must progress through natural stages to develop into healthy, effective teams, each with a common focus and a strong sense of identity. However, the process can be accelerated by structured activity on the part of their manager, aided if desired by a facilitator.

For that reason teambuilding should not be thought of as a 'bolt-on' extra. It is a necessary part of managing a workgroup in such a way that the group comes to recognize the need for more effective teamwork as a *means* of improving its performance. The process is practical, action-centred and focused on real issues that are inhibiting performance, and does not need to be a threatening experience for those involved.

Teambuilding never really comes to an end. In a healthy team it is an extension of the way they work and happens whenever there is a 'felt' need. In the right conditions it can be progressed unaided but will often require the help of an outside facilitator. Whilst the latter can help, the responsibility for the outcome always rests with the manager and the team.

In Part I we have seen how groups develop and grow, and what teambuilding involves. Armed with this understanding we can now go on to examine how to set about designing and running an effective teambuilding programme.

Part II—Designing and running teambuilding programmes

Introduction

From the discussion of the models presented in Part I a picture should be emerging of the ground that will need to be covered and the potential problems to be encountered during the course of a teambuilding programme. Part II concentrates on creating an appropriate design and facilitating the team sessions.

Unlike a knowledge- or skills-based training programme the input in a teambuilding session comes from the participants, and the skill of the facilitator or manager is in creating a simple framework and a climate that will encourage open and constructive debate. This is easily stated but with some teams can be very hard to achieve. You are dealing with actual working groups and the risks if it goes wrong can be high. A clumsy design or badly facilitated session can cause damage to the team or to members within it. Any mistakes made cannot be easily swept aside. They will be carried back into the working environment and will affect ongoing relationships within the team.

For this reason the issues in Part II are covered in some depth. To be forewarned is to be forearmed and, whilst you cannot always predict what will happen on the day, good preparation and planning will significantly increase your ability to deal with the unexpected. What follows is based on many years of hard won experience and the aim of this section is to pass on that experience in the form of practical advice and simple techniques.

Where do you start?

Teambuilding is concerned with change – change from a current identified situation to a required, different state of affairs. The start point of any programme, therefore, must be in diagnosing the current situation within the team and identifying the issues reducing effectiveness.

The first question to be asked is *why* teambuilding seems to be the desired solution. It is all too easy for a manager to feel something is wrong, arrange a day off-site with the team and *then* decide how to use it. A full diagnosis of the situation will determine if teambuilding is the right answer to the team's problems. There are, however, a number of simple questions that a manager or facilitator can consider to test the manager's initial thinking, as follows:

- To what extent does the group *need* to be a team?
- What are their problems: as seen by the leader; and as seen by the team members?
- What is the current climate in the group and how ready are they to participate in a teambuilding programme?
- Does the process of teambuilding basically fit with the leader's style of management?
- What is it realistic to aim at: in the short term; and in the long term?
- How can the manager best validate the answers to the above questions (i.e., what method of diagnosis is needed)?
- To what extent does the manager feel he will need the help of a facilitator?
- Are the manager and the team prepared to put in the time and effort required?

The answers to these questions should help the manager decide if a teambuilding programme is appropriate and if a fuller diagnosis is needed. They will also provide some idea as to what the start point might be: for example, concentrating on objectives and roles; or working on meeting or decision-making processes. Also highlighted will be the extent to which the manager *knows* what the specific problems are or just feels that the situation could be better. It may well be that the problems lie with a single member and therefore will be better addressed on a personal rather than a group basis.

Once you have decided that a teambuilding programme is appropriate there are four stages (summarized in Figure 7) you need to work through to set up and run any sessions, as follows:

- Step 1   Diagnosis
- Step 2   Design and planning
- Step 3   Running the session
- Step 4   Follow-up

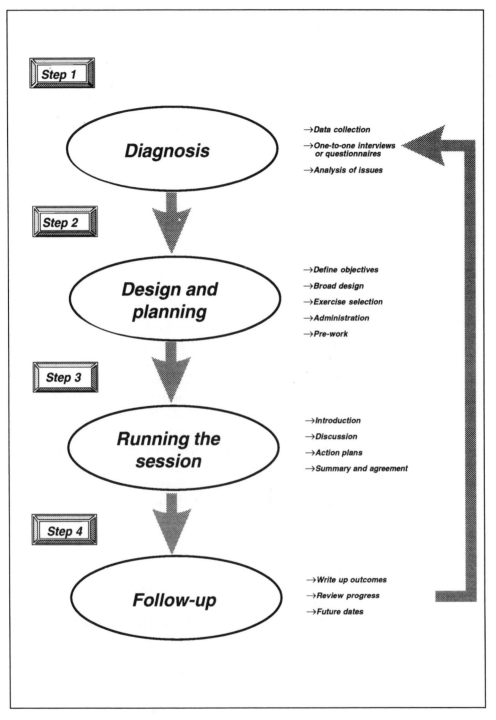

Figure 7: Designing and running workshops

1 | Diagnosis

In answering the list of questions in the Introduction to Part II the manager will have clarified his or her own perception of the current situation. This, however, may be very different from the team's perception and will need to be validated.

The two most commonly used methods for collecting team data are questionnaires and one-to-one discussion with individuals (see Part III, Exercise 1). A typical questionnaire will pose a series of questions that cover the broad aspects of an effective team such as communications, decision making, clarity of objectives, leadership style etc. Similar ground would be covered in one-to-one discussions with individuals but the situation will allow for discussion in depth on particular points. Each technique has advantages and disadvantages, as detailed in Table 1. The method used is a matter of judgement but will depend upon factors such as:

- The openness of the relationship between the manager and individuals in the team.
- The time-scales to which the manager is working.
- The number of individuals involved.

For example, if the relationship between the manager and the team is less than open, a questionnaire used anonymously may generate more honest data. Equally, if the session involves two teams of eight, 16 interviews of about 1–1½ hours may be too time consuming.

If time permits, the best method is one-to-one discussion. **42** Questionnaires do not allow members to qualify their answers and

Table 1: Diagnosis of team issues

Method	Advantages	Disadvantages
Questionnaire	– Quick	– Answers cannot be qualified
	– Conducted anonymously can provide data in sensitive situation	– Individuals are directed to answer a question on an issue that may not be important to them
	– Can be used to collect data across a wide population, including perspectives from customers, subordinates and other interfacing departments	– Provides a snapshot only
	– Easy to collate and present back quantitatively	– Open to misinterpretation and assumptions that cannot be tested
	– Allows quick confirmation of initial thoughts	– Hard to gauge real depth of individual feeling
	– Reduces opportunity for bias if written objectively	– Some individuals may fear putting something in writing
	– Can be less threatening	– Can be filled in to tell the manager what he wants to hear
	– Can be repeated over time – providing an ongoing measure of improvement	– Questions may be misinterpreted if poorly written
		– May raise unduly high expectations of change
One-to-one discussion	– Quality data can be obtained and strength of feeling gauged	– Time consuming
	– Individual concerns and issues can be explored fully	– Good data dependent on an open relationship between manager and team if conducted by the former
	– Using a facilitator, otherwise hidden issues may be voiced	– Harder to ensure same ground covered in all interviews and to the same depth
	– Individuals can be reassured as to what will happen with the data	– Harder to collate the data
	– Discussions can relieve possible tensions by the very fact that a concern has been aired	

do not necessarily reveal the depth of feeling. For example, six out of eight team members may believe team meetings could be improved when asked, but only two may feel it is a big enough issue to want to do something about it.

An interesting variation on both the above, that combines both techniques, is to give out a questionnaire as pre-work for the discussion. This at least alerts people and helps them to structure their thoughts on specific subjects.

The interviews can be undertaken by the manager or a facilitator. One benefit of the manager conducting the interviews is that, as a result of him or her sitting down asking questions about the performance of the team and listening to the interviewee's reply, the teambuilding process has already started! What is critical, however, if the manager conducts the discussions, is that he or she *listens* and does not start defending or disagreeing with the interviewee. The manager's role is to understand; discussions should be reserved for the team session.

If a facilitator is used, his or her role can be one of conducting the one-to-one discussions or designing and collating the results of a questionnaire. A neutral ear can be very beneficial at this stage of the teambuilding process, particularly if the leader is part of the problem, or the feelings of frustration or suspicion are high. Should the facilitator also help to run the team sessions, the one-to-one sessions will serve to develop early rapport between the facilitator and the team. This is very important if the facilitator is external and unknown to the team. However, if the facilitator is internal, trust and credibility must exist already if the data collected are to be meaningful. Finally, the role of any facilitator must be properly communicated, as must the use of the data he or she will collect. It is usual that all personal views given are treated in confidence and only the broad conclusions shared with the leader.

Good data collection and diagnosis is a vital precursor to a successful teambuilding programme. For this is the primary vehicle for ensuring that the right issues are being addressed in the right way. It also reinforces the overall purpose of the teambuilding programme and the role that any facilitator has been asked to play.

2 | Design and planning

The diagnosis carried out will highlight the issues that need to be addressed by your teambuilding programme. There are a number of underlying design principles, however, that must be borne in mind when deciding on the specific programme objectives and design. These principles are summarized in Figure 8, and are detailed as follows:

- **There is no one, right design**. There is no repeatable formula that will work in every circumstance. What may work well with one group, may have less success with another.
- **The structure and design are only a framework**. What is important is the quality of the discussion. The initial design may well need to be dropped or changed during the session if it is more productive to do so.
- **The exercises chosen represent a means to an end**. They are only the stimuli to a constructive, problem-solving discussion. The sophistication of the exercise does not necessarily equate with the quality of the outcome. Timed correctly, a single question may prove more fruitful than a questionnaire that has taken 20 minutes to fill in and share.
- **The design and choice of exercises should help encourage openness and reduce any perceived risk**. Timing the use of an exercise within a session or ongoing programme can have a substantial impact on how much it helps achievement of the objectives. For example, if the group is not ready to be open, a checklist or a questionnaire with penetrating questions may produce little response. Timed correctly, it could lead to two

- There is no one right design

- Structure and design are only a framework; quality of discussion is more important

- Chosen exercises are only a means to an end; go for simplicity and flexibility

- Design and exercise choice should encourage openness and reduce perceived risk

- The group will need to 'warm up'; the design and content should reflect this

- Teambuilding is not done *to* people but *with* them; set realistic objectives

- The design must reflect the diagnosis and the current stage of the group's development

Figure 8: Design principles

hours of constructive debate on a long-standing issue that you wish the group to explore.

- **It takes time for the group to 'warm up' and the design should reflect that fact**. Asking two individuals directly, half an hour into the session, why they avoid each other is not going to be well received! The design should show a natural progression from impersonal issues (e.g. group objectives) to more personal issues (e.g. conflicts in style and behaviour). By the time the latter is ready to be discussed, the group should have settled and be able to talk more freely.

- **Teambuilding is not something you do to people**. It is something they willingly participate in and to that extent, the pace and what is achieved is self-regulating. This point should be evident in both the objectives and the design ambitions. Quite often if the timing, setting and approach are right, the leader's expectations can be exceeded.

– **The design _must_ take account of both the diagnosis and the current stage of the group's development**. Properly done teambuilding will accelerate the development of the group through the 'forming' to 'performing' stage (see Chapter 2, 'How does a group develop?'). However, the process cannot be rushed and stages bypassed – to do so will only mean the group eventually having to retrace its steps. For example, pushing through decisions on meeting structures whilst the group is only at the second stage will merely cover up any dissent. This dissent will inevitably be raised in both overt and covert ways in the future until it is addressed properly. At the same time, the opening up of the team 'arena' (see Chapter 2, 'How are trust and openness developed?') can be encouraged by a good design but not forced. Having the right level of patience with 'slower' members of the group can be a real test for the leader who knows what it feels like to work in a healthy, open team.

With these ground rules in mind, there are five sets of activities to work through in designing and preparing for each session – bearing in mind the need may be for a single session or a series of sessions that build upon each other. At each stage, you will need to answer a number of key questions.

The five sets of activities are: deciding the objectives and broad content; mapping out the design; exercise selection; administration; and pre-work.

Deciding the objectives and broad content

At this point it is essential not to be over-ambitious. Depending on the number of issues, the extent to which they relate to goals, roles, processes or relationships, and the prevailing climate of openness in the team, the first question to be answered is: 'Can the issues be addressed fully in a single session?' If they cannot – and that is very much a matter of judgement – the question then is: 'What should be the initial step?' The hierarchy of goals, roles, processes and relationships provides a good, safe framework within which to consider progress (see Part I, 'What are the main problems encountered by teams?').

For example, if the team is clear as to its goals, the leader may start the session off with a short presentation on those goals in order to set the scene and move straight into syndicate work or discussion on how the team needs to operate to achieve them. If the team is new, they may well spend a full day sharing perspectives and agreeing the team's goals, with no time on other issues such as how they will need to meet or communicate. These points can be covered at a second session.

It is better when setting objectives to keep them broad. For example:

- To develop a common understanding of the challenges facing the department over the next 12 months.
- To gain common understanding and commitment to the overall purpose and role of the team.
- To review the effectiveness of our meeting structures and process.

Keeping them broad allows flexibility when running the session. If issues are raised that are significant and it makes sense to progress them at that time, the group and leader will find it easier to adapt the agenda. This will be helped if the leader considers in advance what success will look like at the end of the session – in maximum and minimum terms. What is the most and the least he or she could hope for?

A teambuilding session is to some extent an unknown quantity. Good diagnosis and design are the best way of ensuring that the real needs of the group are worked on, but it is common for undisclosed issues, often deeply felt, to be raised by members during the session. To deal summarily with, or even dismiss, such issues because the team has a design that does not include discussion on them, belies the whole spirit of teambuilding. Similarly, it is easy to become disappointed and feel a sense of failure when the leader is too determined on a single definition of success. He or she has only two options – to achieve it or not. Groups can be unpredictable and may, for some apparently unknown reason at the time, appear to be held up on one subject. Usually the reason is a hidden agenda or lack of skill within the group.

In a short team session, time can often appear to pass with little obvious progress being made. Having a range of success in mind will help the leader to allow time in such situations for the hidden agenda to be aired, whilst still feeling progress is being made.

If the teambuilding programme is aimed at a wider group than the leader's immediate subordinates, the leader at this stage must also decide the level of attendance required to achieve the objectives. This can be a difficult decision for the leader who must balance the inclusion of individuals against the total size of the group. A large group is going to find it harder to manage its process on the day, whilst exclusion of individuals can build up resistance or resentment. In most cases, the attendance is almost self-selecting and the problem is one of developing a design to fit the group size selected. (The implications of handling different group sizes is covered later in this chapter.)

In summary then, the main decisions made at this stage are as follows:

- Does it require a single session or an ongoing programme?
- What are the broad objectives of the session? What will success look like – minimum/maximum?
- Who should attend?

It is necessary to be flexible and not overly ambitious, and to think in terms of a strategy as opposed to a 'quick fix'. The development of a group does take time. The design and the activities for the group, which the programme demands, need to be consistent with the state of development of the group. If they are not, this situation is likely to result in a difficult session and awkwardness on the day.

Mapping out the design

Having decided on the overall strategy and the outline content in terms of issues to work on, the leader can now decide the following:

- The length of session needed.
- Whether the session is on- or off-site.
- The broad timetable and basic design.

Duration and location

The length of the session needed, and whether to hold it off-site or on-site, depend on a number of factors:

- At what stage during the programme is that particular planned event – the initial event or otherwise?
- The climate and skills existing in the team and their past experience of teambuilding.
- The amount of ground to be covered and how difficult or easy it is likely to be to reach agreements.
- The nature of the issues to be covered and the extent to which they are personal.
- How much it will cost and the ease with which the whole team can be released from their jobs.

At the start of a teambuilding programme an initial workshop of 2–3 days is likely to be needed, with ongoing sessions of 1–1½ days over the next 6 months. By the time two or three sessions have been run – except with a particularly difficult group – this could be reduced to sessions of 1–1½ days every 6 months. With a taskforce or project team that has a reasonably short life of 6–12 months, it is likely that the initial session will need to be 3–5 days. This is because the group needs to sort out the issues of goals, roles and processes very quickly, and may well need some input on skills such as communication, presentations, meetings etc.

As regards location, if issues need full debate or the session is the first of a series, it is always best to run the session 'off-site' or away from the job, budget permitting. For a management team, this is likely to be in a local hotel. For a shopfloor taskforce, it could be in the company's training suite. To gain real value from the investment, the team must focus its energies solely on the workshop. On-site teambuilding sessions are fraught with late arrivals, interruptions and difficulties in keeping the group together during breaks and meal times. This is particularly so with management teams – *be warned!* With operator teams who have not been exposed to working away from the department, the difference of using a training centre or other meeting facilities may be sufficient to help them to concentrate solely on the objectives. The nature of their jobs also means that outside interruptions are unlikely – unless of course you are working with the only group of service electricians on site when there is a power failure!

Bear in mind that with on-site sessions of longer than a day's duration, individuals will go home overnight and the momentum of the meeting will be broken. Your next day's design will therefore need to allow for a slow start. With off-site sessions where individuals stay overnight this is not a problem. The benefits of overnight stays and keeping the group together to socialize can go a long way to helping solve or progress issues. It also means that if at the end of the first day the group is really opening up, they can work on into the evening if they wish. When working with the group during the 'storming' stage, taking them off-site can help considerably, if for no other reason than that it represents neutral territory.

This is not to say that teambuilding cannot be done on-site. Budget alone may prevent the use of outside facilities. If it is done on-site, however, you must be aware of the disadvantages and adjust both the objectives and the design, and plan to minimize predictable problems.

As a final point, for teams that have reached the 'norming' and 'performing' stages, location presents less of a problem. By then the group will be better disciplined and place sufficient value on team sessions that they will concentrate on the task in hand and not allow interruptions to cause problems.

In high performing teams, team reviews are very much part of the normal process of working together. They may simply be tagged on to the end of a business meeting or conducted in quiet areas in the workplace. Such a team, however, may still wish to go off-site if the agenda will take a day or more (e.g. developing a new set of objectives for the next year).

Broad timetable and basic design

Having decided the duration and location of the session, a broad timetable of the event needs to be formulated to test whether the objectives are achievable in the time allowed. This is simpler than it seems since all team sessions will include natural breaks for lunch, tea etc., which divide the day into discrete time slots. There will also need to be an introduction, some sort of exercise to get the group started and a review of the workshop at the end.

As can be seen from the examples in Figure 9, this leaves a number of defined blocks of time in which the group will work against the objectives. The longer the session, the more blocks of time are available. In this way the examples illustrated represent crude templates to work from when designing the detail. These should *not,* however, be used as rigid formulas, but more as loose structures around which to arrange the activities. As confidence increases in facilitating teambuilding sessions, so you will need less and less structure. Some of the most fruitful discussions can come from a well-timed, simple question and the ensuing, free-flowing discussion that can run on straight through any planned break. Choosing what to put into the separate sessions on the workshop is determined from the objectives, bearing in mind the broad principles outlined at the start of this section and the hierarchy of issues explained in Part I (i.e. goal, roles etc.).

The sessions in the structures illustrated in Figure 9 have been numbered. This does not necessarily mean that they should each be used to tackle a separate issue. For example, in the 1-day event, all the sessions could be to do with development of objectives. For example:

- Session 1   Syndicate working
- Session 2   Presentation and discussion
- Sessions 3/4   Paired working – action planning against objectives agreed in Session 2.

51

1-day event
(8 hours)

Introduction	15 min
Warm-up exercise	30 min
Session 1	1 hr
Break	15 min
Session 2	2 hrs
Lunch	
Session 3	1 hr
Break	15 min
Session 4	1 hr
Summary and review of day	15 min

Half-day event
(4 hours)

Warm-up exercise	30 min
Session 1	1.5 hrs
Break	15 min
Session 2	1.5 hrs
Conclusions/summary Review of session	} 15 min

1½ to 3-day event

Day 1 (commences 4.00 p.m.)

Introduction	15 min
Warm-up exercise	1 hr
Session 1	1.5 hrs
Dinner	

(Possible continuation of Session 1 or overnight preparation)

Day 2,3 etc.

Structure as the 1-day session without warm-up exercise.

Notes

– On short events of ½–1 day's duration, time will always be tight – try not to tackle too many different issues at once. With sessions of 1½ days and beyond, the 'getting started' phase is out of the way on the first afternoon, giving the chance for a lot of ground to be covered on the full days following.

– Use breaks to provide natural pauses or conclusions in the team's conversations, allowing changes in direction and providing time to assess how the session is going.

– If the events of 1½ days or more are run 'on-site' include some mechanism for recapitulating on the previous day and warming-up the group after the introduction on days 2,3 etc..

Figure 9: Design templates

The natural flow should commence with broader, impersonal topics (e.g. objectives, broad discussion on what the organization does well or not so well) and move on to more personalized topics (e.g., feedback on individual behaviours) as the group becomes more and more open and comfortable with the process. You can almost consider the process like peeling off the layers of an onion. Some issues may be voiced on several occasions – each time the speaker reveals more of what he or she really thinks and becomes increasingly specific in his or her comments.

A clumsy design can place people in a very uncomfortable position early on, which could cause them to withdraw from discussion or become unnecessarily defensive. Part of the skill is in designing and linking the separate sessions so that the overall design fosters the processes of self-disclosure, feedback and risk taking. In a good design, this pattern is seen to repeat itself both within a single workshop and across a series of workshops.

The outcome of all these deliberations will be a set of achievable objectives and an outline programme reflecting the diagnosis and the current stage of the group's development. A simple example is illustrated in Figure 10.

Exercise selection

Having developed a broad design, with the aims of the various sections within it roughly sketched out, it is now possible to decide what exercises and methods should be used for each individual section.

Until you are experienced in designing programmes this step must follow the broad design. The temptation is to pick exercises that have worked well in the past, perhaps with other teams, and apply them to the present team. But the exercises are *not* an end in themselves. They are simply there to help the group get into constructive debate, reduce any perceived risks and encourage openness and feedback. The worst possible teambuilding designs look like back-to-back exercises representing the leader's or the facilitator's all-time favourites! Figure 11 shows the main headings to be considered in planning the use of exercises.

The details of various exercises that can be used are the subject of Part III, where their application and the timing of their use are fully covered. There are, however, a few general points of principle, relating to the overall design, that are worth covering at this stage, as follows:

53

Objectives

- To review the challenges facing us during the next 12 months - agreeing priorities

- To review how we are operating as a team, identifying the main areas for improvement

- To agree actions to progress issues

Broad design

- Introduction

- Warm-up exercise

- Session 1

  - Challenges for the next 12 months
  - Presentation by leader/ initial questions

    Break

- Session 2

  - Discussion on objectives - hopes/fears
  - Agree priority areas
  - Agree action plan to prepare specific objectives

    Lunch

- Session 3

  - Review team effectiveness - goods/bads

    Break

- Session 4

  - Agree priority areas for increasing team performance
  - Agree actions to address/ progress main issues

- Summary of day/actions

- Review of day - likes/dislikes etc

Figure 10: Example of workshop design

- Use simple exercises – maximize discussion

- Build in variety

- Be flexible with exercise timescales

- Remember outcomes can be variable and not always predictable

- Complicated exercises can deflect discussion

- Anticipate where the group may get stuck and time lost

- Match breaks in the exercise with natural breaks

- Plan 'activity' after lunch

Figure 11: Using exercises

- **Keep the exercise simple and maximize the discussion**. Cumbersome exercises that require much individual work on the day may just slow down the discussion and make it harder to get it started again.
- **Be flexible with the timescales**. Plan in 'slack time'. If the day is timed to the minute, with exercises squeezed in, you can guarantee that you will get behind.
- **Do not believe that if an exercise has worked several times before and produced quality outputs that it always will**. They sometimes do not, without any easily explicable reason.
- **Some people will deflect discussion if the exercise is too complicated**. They can get tense and irritable about statistical norms or the rationale behind a questionnaire scoring, for example, and lose the basic point of what the exercise is trying to lead the group into.
- **Consider where the group may be held up and where time is likely to be lost on the day**. Think through how you would change the rest of the design if that happened. In particular,

55

think what you might leave out. Doing this now will relieve some of the pressure on the day if this situation occurs.

- **Link natural breaks in the day (e.g. tea, coffee etc.) to the steps of the exercise**. For example, time a tea break for the end of syndicate working, with presentations starting straight afterwards.
- **Watch out for the 'graveyard shift' straight after lunch when people will be naturally sleepy**. Plan in an active exercise for that session as opposed to a presentation or a film.

This stage of designing the event runs parallel with development of the broad design. Exercises may need to be modified or changed for the workshop to fit into the timescale available, or the broad design and times changed if a particular exercise needs to be run but cannot be modified.

As you become skilled in designing events, the two steps will merge into one. As you are thinking through the broad design, particular exercises will already be shaping up in your mind. Do not squeeze exercises into time slots that are unrealistic, for this only results in hurrying the group unnecessarily – better to modify the exercise, simplifying a questionnaire or using buzz groups instead of syndicate exercises.

Administration

Once a detailed design has been developed, it becomes clear what facilities and equipment are needed (e.g. number of rooms, OHP, flip charts etc.). The following points are worth making, however, which will help the running of the team session on the day:

- Make sure the main room is suitable. It should be a good size to allow the group to be seated around a single or U-shaped table and still provide space for small groups to pull their chairs together whilst working in buzz groups or pairs. It should be light and airy – ideally with windows to the outside. Too often hotels locate meetings in converted bedrooms with minimum light and only a few inches of space between the seated delegates and the walls of the room. This may be suitable for a 4-hour business meeting with 3 or 4 people, or as a syndicate room used for short periods; but as a main room in a teambuilding session it will be a real handicap, creating a depressing and dismal atmosphere from the start. For a session of 5 or 6 individuals, the *minimum* room size should be 25' x 25'. This gives room for equipment, buzz group working or individual working with flipchart paper.

- Keep the syndicate rooms as near to the main room as possible. Much time can be lost with sub-groups wandering to and fro between rooms. This is particularly so for the facilitator who is trying to spend time with each group during syndicate sessions.
- Try to arrange coffee breaks to be laid out in a different area rather than in the main room. It is good to take the group on occasions into a different environment. Being in the same room for 4 or 5 hours at a stretch can become wearing and concentration will slip.
- Try to find a hotel that has quiet public areas which could be used for paired or individual working.
- If the session requires overnight stays, find a hotel where it will be easy and comfortable for the group to stay together and socialize. Many hotels in towns have very poor public areas and are excessively noisy. With this type of hotel, it is often better to keep the group together by eating out rather than in the hotel restaurant. To this extent many of the smaller, country hotels can provide an ideal environment.
- If you are hiring equipment such as a video recorder make sure that you use a reliable hirer, particularly if the use of the equipment is critical to the design of the workshop. There is nothing worse than arriving to find the microphone does not work or is unsuitable and the hotel has no back-up.

The above comments may seem over-particular but the location and facilities really can have a marked effect on the underlying atmosphere in the session, either helping or seriously detracting from it. They are variables within the teambuilding process, but ones which with some forethought can easily be managed to advantage.

A fuller checklist of preparation for a workshop, including more obvious comments, is shown in Figure 12.

Pre-work

As the time available on a workshop is always likely to be limited, it is useful to consider work that can be done by the group or members before they arrive. This could take the form of some simple questions concerning team performance for people to think through (see Part III, Exercise 2 for a typical list), or presentations to be prepared on specific inputs required.

Pre-work instructions will need to be sent out in advance, along with a joining letter detailing the objectives and hotel arrangements. You may want to include a simple programme if the session

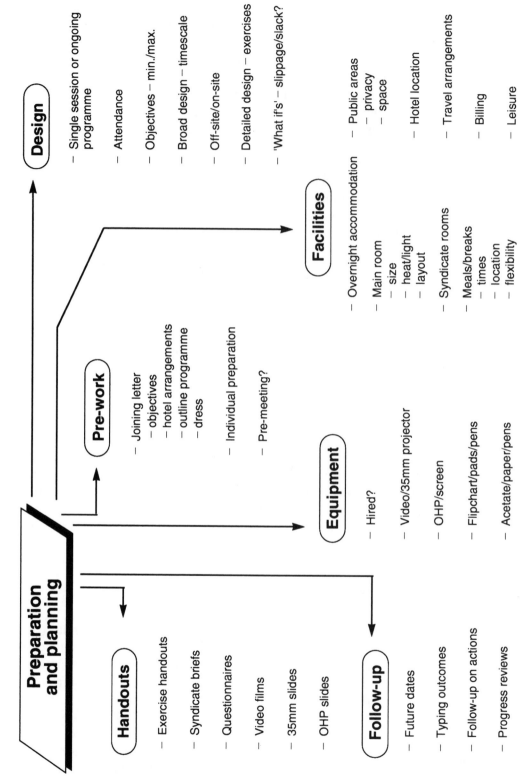

Figure 12: Preparation checklist for teambuilding

is running over a number of days. Given that you will want maximum flexibility on the day, it is probably not advisable to send out your own detailed design. This will help to avoid possible arguments as to 'why are we doing something different?' when you make changes during the session.

This again is a matter of personal judgement, however. You may feel the particular group needs a detailed plan to help remove any fear of the unknown. For example, a session with a project team of operators who have been brought together for a short project and have no previous experience of teambuilding or off-site sessions will probably welcome more details before arriving. With a very nervous group you may even consider a short pre-meeting to explain the objectives of the day, what is likely to happen and to explain any pre-work required.

The proper design and planning of a teambuilding programme based on an initial diagnosis will go a long way towards ensuring a successful workshop. Keep it simple, and throughout your preparation continually ask the question: 'Will this design provide the right opportunity for the problems to be constructively aired and addressed?'

The preceding sections may seem like a daunting task to those who have never run a teambuilding session, but most of it is logical and common sense. And if followed, it will help *pre-empt* possible problems on the day. As stated previously, the more experienced you become at facilitating sessions the less will be your need for structure. What structure does is provide support. What it must *not* be allowed to do is prevent flexibility or inhibit discussion.

With clear objectives, a simple framework for the session and an understanding of the issues that will probably be raised, you will be well prepared to tackle the programme. This, however, represents only half the picture. The other half, which is the subject of the next section, is the skill of facilitating and handling the individual sessions.

3 | Running the session

The consequences of a badly handled teambuilding session with a working team can be potentially serious for their ongoing working relationships. Once something has been said in the heat of the moment it cannot be retracted. The facilitator's aim is to create an environment in which individuals will open up and increase their own self-awareness by accepting feedback – an environment in which people feel helped rather than attacked.

Forewarning of potential arguments and sensitivities, and a knowledge of the leader and the team, will all help, but you must be clear as to your role at each session and be skilled in handling group situations. What follows is designed to offer some solutions to the following issues:

- The role of the manager and/or facilitator.
- How to ensure constructive discussions.
- How to tackle some of the more predictable problems, such as dominant or quiet individuals, hidden agendas etc.

The role of the manager and/or facilitator

If the manager uses a facilitator, the latter's role is simply stated as 'managing the process', which includes the following responsibilities:

- Creating the right climate for participation and discussion.
- Keeping the group focused on the objectives.

- Adjusting the design, where necessary.
- Helping the group confront issues constructively.
- Helping the group crystallize its thinking and develop clear conclusions and actions.
- Managing the physical environment (i.e. the hotel, equipment etc.).

The facilitator does *not* contribute to the 'content'. In other words, whatever agreements and conclusions are reached, say about future meeting structures or decision-making levels, they are the group's *own* conclusions. It is not the facilitator's place to advise on the best meeting structure or who should take what decisions. The facilitator's role is solely concerned with helping the group identify such issues and making sure that *they* resolve them to *their* satisfaction.

The only input a facilitator will make to the content of any discussion would be of a training nature. For example, he or she may outline the criteria for a good objective, or a checklist against which to review meeting effectiveness etc. Such input can then be used by the group to help them make quality decisions and choices.

When a facilitator is used, the manager, having agreed the design for the workshop, need only open and close the session. For the remainder of the time, he or she can concentrate on being an active participant, and can worry less about how the day is progressing or whether the administrative arrangements are working. Needless to say, this does require trust between the facilitator and the manager. The facilitator requires the freedom to adjust or change the programme so that the objectives are met and to be able to do this without immediate reference to the manager; though a good facilitator will be checking throughout the session on how the manager is feeling and helping him or her to understand what is happening.

The relationship between the manager and the facilitator is very important. It is, after all, the manager's session and he or she must be comfortable with the outcome. Equally though, there is nothing more frustrating for a facilitator than to be given a job and not allowed to do it.

Without outside help the manager will need to take on two roles – that of the facilitator and that of a participant. This is not always easy for the following two reasons:

- Managing the 'process' of the day requires conscious thought and standing back from any discussion to view what is going on (e.g. Are all contributing? How is the time going? Is the design working? What is the issue that is blocking progress? etc.).

- Changing frequently between roles can confuse the rest of the group who will start to be unsure at times which role the manager is playing.

One of the other problems for the manager when playing the role of facilitator is how he or she introduces a personal view on a particular subject. Stating it firmly and then asking for the rest of the group's views may not always elicit honest answers, especially if the relationship is not a comfortable one or the manager is viewed as autocratic. As explained below, when leading a discussion, the leader should *add* his or her views to those of the group and must be careful not to abuse his or her position as leader by dominating the group with those views. It is possible for the manager to facilitate *and* act as a participant, provided he or she consciously works at it and explains this dual role to the group at the beginning. The problem is minimal when the group is at the 'forming', 'norming' and 'performing' stages (see Part I, 'How does a group develop?'). At the forming stage, the group will not feel overly threatened by the leader providing direction – indeed they may welcome it. At the later stages, the trust levels and collaboration that exist will mean that the group is comfortable with this double role, or if it causes a problem, will feel able to say so.

The difficult stage is when the group is 'storming'. During this stage, trust is at its lowest and the leader's role is often being challenged. If the issues to be tackled are those associated with this stage of the group's development, help in the form of a facilitator is recommended. Equally, if the manager wants to contribute heavily to the content of the discussions – for example, agreeing objectives, or deciding authority levels – he or she may want to release the added burden of managing the process to a facilitator.

How to ensure constructive discussions

Central to the process of teambuilding sessions is the group discussion: *the sharing of ideas and feelings with a view to gaining some form of agreement*. Thus the manager or facilitator must understand the mechanics of handling a discussion, the pitfalls they can fall into and the common problems encountered.

For example, the team may have spent time in two syndicates reviewing the effectiveness of their meetings. They have presented their thoughts and have identified one or two areas they need to cover in order to reach agreement on such matters as meeting attendance or frequency – and they have decided to do this by open discussion.

The discussion processes they must follow are demonstrated in Figure 13. This model identifies four distinct stages which together form the discussion 'loop'.

Stage 1 – Introduce the subject

The discussion leader introduces the subject that the group is about to discuss, by summarizing the two or three issues to be debated and explaining that, over say the next 30 minutes, he or she wants the group to reach agreement on what changes they need to make. The decisive step at this stage is to hand the subject over to the group and get them talking.

The unskilful leader, however, will immediately voice his or her view and ask what others think – wrong! This is a guaranteed way to suppress the views of others, especially if the discussion leader happens to be the team leader. If the discussion leader is the facilitator, he or she should *not* be influencing the group with personal views of what should be done anyway!

Stage 2 – Pass the subject to the group

In many ways this is the hardest part for the discussion leader. He or she needs to ensure that all the team members have a chance to

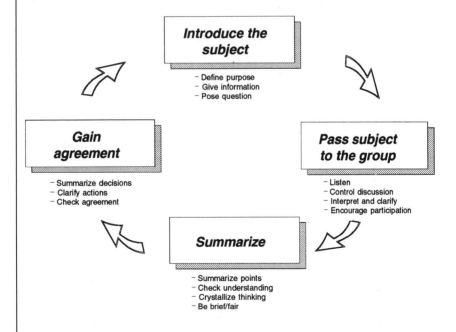

63 | **Figure 13:** The discussion loop

voice their views, bringing in the quieter members and controlling the dominant ones. It may also be difficult to get the group started and it may be necessary to draw in others deliberately (e.g. 'Bill, what do you think?').

This stage can often appear messy, with lots of ideas and alternatives being put forward, but if it is over-structured by the discussion leader it will inhibit free discussion. A simple analogy would be a referee in a football match. A good referee is hardly noticed and the game flows freely, with just sufficient control to keep it on track and not let it get out of hand. A bad referee is blowing the whistle for every minor infringement. The net effect is that the game becomes very 'stop–start' and never really gets going. The quality of the overall game in each situation is self-evident, and so it is with a discussion that is over-controlled.

The discussion leader's role during this stage is summarized as follows:

- Listening.
- Controlling the discussion.
- Interpreting and clarifying.
- Encouraging participation.

This process can be especially difficult for a team leader who may well have strong personal views on the subject. Circumstances require that he or she should put those views to one side and remain neutral. For a neutral facilitator this is clearly not a problem – though it can be sorely tempting at times to tell the group what they should do or to take sides in the argument! Being dismissive, putting down others' ideas and arguing are not the behaviours required of the leader here. A good discussion leader is able to put his or her own thoughts to one side and concentrate on 'managing the process' – helping members to explain themselves, helping to resolve differences of view, reducing conflict and tension, and ensuring individuals get a fair chance to speak.

This step can also be difficult when hidden agendas are present (see below) and people are hiding their true feelings (e.g. 'If the boss would only turn up on time for meetings, there would not be a problem getting through the agenda!').

Stage 3 – Summarize

After a period of time – say, 10 to 30 minutes – the leader should halt the discussion and summarize where he or she thinks the discussion is up to. As most people are not skilled, succinct communicators, it will not be unusual for the previous 15 minutes or so of lively debate to result in only two or three main points being made and these can be summed up in a few sentences.

This stage is imperative, however, for three reasons: to ensure that the discussion is focused and stays on track; to test that all understand what has been said; and to prevent members being left behind in the process. It may well become obvious during the summary that one or two people are still unclear on a certain point, and this will give the leader an opportunity to go back a stage and re-open the discussion on that point. This is also a pivotal stage when there are strongly conflicting views within the group. Through summarizing, the leader can regain control of the discussion if it is becoming too heated and can isolate the different viewpoints, which can then be worked on and reconciled (e.g. 'so, what you are saying, Fred, is . . .' and 'what you are saying Jo is . . . If we can resolve that issue . . .'.).

At this point, the leader and the group may need to make decisions on the direction of the discussion. For example, discussion on meeting attendance may well have led the group into a debate on team membership. During the summary stage the team will need to decide whether to continue discussion on team membership or stay with the original subject of meetings. It may be that the group will decide to postpone further discussion on team membership until a later date, or, conversely, may feel that it is sufficiently important to merit closing the discussion on meetings for now and changing the line of the debate.

Without proper summary, most discussions will get held up or side-tracked, causing feelings of frustration for all. Too frequent summary, however, will inhibit free flow of discussion in the same way as the bad referee mentioned above. The skill of the discussion leader is to balance the amount of summary against the freedom of discussion.

Stage 4 – Gain agreement

This final step in the discussion effectively closes the 'loop' and, to some extent, merges with stage 3 in that it is a form of summary.

Having allowed free flow of discussion on the chosen subject and summarized points emerging from it, the leader has finally to test agreement to decisions made and actions proposed. It is important to do this before moving on to the next subject (or perhaps, in a team session, to a totally different activity). Testing agreement slows the process down and helps to ensure that all members have a common understanding of what decisions and actions they are agreeing to. It allows a 'second chance' after the main discussion for members to test their personal commitment and comfort with what has been agreed. In this way, follow-up actions have a better chance of happening.

The above, then, is the discussion 'loop' – a constructive way for a group to debate and agree actions against issues raised. If four or five issues are being debated, you would need to cycle around the loop with each issue. Dependent on the complexity of the issue and the strength of opinion, it can take 10 minutes to 1 hour or more to go around the loop just once! What it does allow you to do, however, is exercise control over the debate in a way that should not restrict individual contribution.

The discussion leader's role can therefore be summed up as follows:

- Managing the process.
- Creating a climate for participation.
- Moving the discussion forward.
- Guiding the group to conclusions and decisions.
- Gaining agreement to action.

Leading the discussion does take conscious effort and requires the leader frequently to stand back from the discussion, looking at what is going on and listening hard. If no one in the group adopts this role – be it the team leader, a designated team member or the facilitator – it is very likely that the discussion will drift, stumble or break down altogether. Lively discussion, on the other hand, properly managed, will produce positive outcomes and a high degree of satisfaction in those participating. Some of the main Do's and Do nots of discussion leadership are summarized in Figure 14.

Avoiding the more predictable problems

In the previous section, we touched on some of the potential difficulties that can get in the way of constructive discussion. In this section we will look more closely at these predictable problems that can occur 'on the day', and which include the following:

- Hidden agendas.
- Handling conflict.
- Dominant and quiet members.
- Warming up groups.

Do's	Do nots
- Plan and prepare	- Allow outside interruption
- Manage the time	- Dominate
- Listen	- Make assumptions
- Acknowledge all ideas	- Give your opinions first
- Avoid inadvertent rejection	- Compete with members
- Reinforce and build on contributions	- Take sides
- Summarize and test understanding regularly	- Immediately focus on flaws in others' arguments
- Encourage participation	- Argue
- Protect the weak	- Manipulate
- Control the strong	- Be dismissive
- Keep the energy high	- Be condescending
- Handle conflict	

. . . be a servant not a master

Figure 14: Discussion leadership

- Large groups and small groups.
- Syndicates and buzz groups.
- Energy levels.

What are these problems and how might they be tackled?

Hidden agendas

Groups work simultaneously and continuously at two levels – on the open agenda and on hidden agendas.

The open agenda

The open agenda is the declared intent and objectives of the meeting or discussion. This is formally labelled and agreed, either verbally at the start of the discussion, or in the form of a written agenda.

The hidden agenda

A hidden agenda is personal to an individual, private and usually not declared. More often than not, it is deeply felt and important to that individual.

For example, consider a team meeting with an open agenda to review allocation of roles on a project. It could well be that one or two members of that team fear that something they like doing will be taken away from them. Another member may be coming to the meeting intent on securing responsibilities for a task or area he or she has wanted for some time. Two others may see themselves as extremely busy and are worrying about being given yet another task to do as a result of the team session. Each of those individuals comes to the meeting with their own personal but hidden agenda that they will work on with or without the team's permission! All these desires, motives or fears are genuine and deeply felt and will affect the behaviour of people during the session. As the open agenda is being discussed, each member will be separately working under cover on their own agenda, trying to ensure that their personal requirements are met.

It must be appreciated that hidden agendas are natural. Too often they are condemned as negative – part of some deliberate, devious plot to subvert the meeting! – but this is rarely the case. Usually they are brought about by some personal anxieties that the individual, for a host of reasons, does not feel able to voice: for example, concern about looking stupid, lack of confidence, or a fear of the unknown etc. In some cases, the person may not even be conscious of his or her hidden agenda!

What is equally clear, however, is that these hidden agendas must be dealt with. For the facilitator or manager running the team session, this is one of the aims of the diagnosis stage of team-building. If the hidden agendas can be discovered at that stage, it will help the facilitator understand what is causing the behaviours they observe during the session. As a result the facilitator will be better placed to help members to voice their concerns in open session. In the worst case, it will help the facilitator to prevent a member overworking his or her own issue to the exclusion of others' needs.

Not all hidden agendas will be discovered before the session. However, if the session is seriously held up on its open agenda, it is very likely to be because some member or members are working their own hidden agendas. For example, an individual may keep trying to lead the group away from discussing a particular issue because he or she does not want to become involved in such a discussion, since it is not in his or her interests to do so.

So what do you do? Here are some practical ideas:

- **Do not view the situation as good or bad. Your objective must be to persuade the person to voice his or her hidden agenda**. Once it is in the open, it can be dealt with. Try to encourage the person to talk about the issue by questioning and probing (e.g. 'You don't seem comfortable with that. Is there a problem?', 'How do you feel about it?' etc.). This has to be done in a non-threatening way. Cornering the individual or deliberately putting them on the spot (e.g. 'It's pretty obvious that you've got a problem with the idea . . .') is not going to be productive.
- **Your role as facilitator is simple. It is to help by understanding and encouraging the other individual to talk**. Sensitivity is key. Possibly the matter is nothing to do with the workplace but may be a domestic problem. Or it may be a work issue that the individual can be encouraged to talk about outside the session: for example, a deep-seated disrespect of another team member, which means that every time that other person puts forward an idea it is rejected by the first person.
- **Dealing with it may not always mean resolving it**. It may be that all you can do at the meeting is to try to understand it and empathize, and you or the team leader will have to take up the matter again outside the session for separate discussion. Agreeing this with the person during the session may be

enough to allow him or her to concentrate again on the open agenda.

A deeply felt issue that is not confronted in this way will sometimes be easily spotted because the individual raises it in a vague way periodically during the session.

Probably the worst situation is when the hidden issue is deeply felt by a number of the team members to the point where it is becoming impossible to progress the open agenda and gain any agreement or decisions. Such situations are infrequent but not unknown, and you have two options: disengage or confront the group. First, disengaging means leaving that part of the open agenda for another day. After the session, the leader can then decide his strategy for getting at the real problems and solving them. This may involve separate discussions with each individual on the matter, that is, further diagnosis. Second, you could stop the meeting working on the open agenda and confront the hidden issue there and then. This is obviously high risk, and how effective the result will be depends very much on the facilitator's or leader's skills and credibility with the team. For a facilitator there is slightly less risk in that he or she is neutral in the matter. If you do decide to confront a group hard during a session, it is imperative that you have your facts right and that your intervention is timed and done skilfully, otherwise the group may collectively turn against you. If the time feels right, however, stopping work on the open agenda and dealing with the hidden agenda may be the exact motivation the group requires to move forward several steps in its development.

A final point to consider, for the team leader especially, is whether the hidden agenda relates to the leadership of the group!

The impact of hidden agendas on team sessions and the ease with which they can be dealt with will vary depending on the stage of the group's development. Clearly in the early stages – 'forming' and 'storming' – it will be harder to resolve them and they can have a serious effect on the productivity of the group. Once into the 'norming' and 'performing' stages, they are fewer because levels of openness and trust are higher and the climate is far more conducive to resolving them simply and quickly.

In summary, the main points to remember about hidden agendas are:

- They are a natural part of the process – neither bad nor good.
- Do not always expect top speed action on the open agenda.
- Help and encourage hidden agendas to be shared so that they may be dealt with.

– Do not corner individuals – be sensitive – tackle them outside the meeting if necessary.

In this way, you have a better chance of turning hidden feelings into positive contribution.

Handling conflict

Diversity of view is again a natural part of the team process. Without it, a group is likely to be complacent, content, and in danger of suppressing individual contribution to a point where the quality of the team's output is lessened. Moreover, the nature of the topics discussed in teambuilding sessions is more than likely to bring out very emphatically those differences of view. Some facilitators contend that without at least one good argument in a teambuilding session, the group is not going to develop!

As with hidden agendas, the role of the facilitator or manager is not to suppress conflict but to bring it out in a way that allows differences of opinion to be handled constructively. Is not the essence of teambuilding shared knowledge and mutual understanding as opposed to continual consensus? Here are a few pointers which will help you to handle conflict when it arises:

– **Work at diffusing the emotion that often accompanies conflict**. Politely question and probe to get at the real source of the conflict – it may have nothing to do with what they are appearing to argue about.
– **Try to isolate the real difference between the opposing views**. Often two people will argue vehemently over a tiny difference of opinion without realizing it. Both people hear only the aggression and tone of the other person's voice, to which they respond in kind.
– **Use summary and clarification of each person's view** as a way of helping to understand the problem for yourself, and more importantly, as a way of getting each person to listen to the other's viewpoint.
– **Having isolated the true difference, test how much it really matters**. Confronted in this way with a logical view, both parties may decide they are arguing over nothing and step down.
– **As with hidden agendas, choose whether to resolve the problem there and then, or agree to deal with it outside the session**. It may be enough for both parties to know that it will be

addressed in due course. If you do this, however, you must follow up the action agreed for the sake of your own credibility.

The underlying principle behind these actions is to de-escalate the conflict by reducing emotions, encouraging listening and gaining clarity and objectivity.

Where you expect conflict at a team session, it may be useful to start the day by agreeing with the group some ground rules on behaviour (see Part III, Exercise 2). These ground rules should focus on how the group needs to work during the day (e.g. listen, give constructive feedback, say what they feel, participate). During the session itself, if the group moves away from these rules, members can be fairly confronted with any negative behaviours. With groups in which members expect emotional conflict, they will often welcome the agreement of a checklist as a form of protection from unfair criticism. Whilst the group should develop their own list, if you are skilful you should be able to use the opportunity to introduce your own 'markers' about acceptable and unacceptable behaviour.

Dominant and quiet members

Excessively dominant and quiet members are perhaps the most common problems encountered on team sessions by a team leader or facilitator.

The two main techniques used for controlling participation during a discussion are 'bringing in' and 'shutting out'.

Bringing in

'Bringing in' controls participation through inclusion, positively inviting the quiet individuals to comment by open questions ('Brian, what's your view?', 'Mary, Fred, you've not commented. What do you think about the idea?').

Some members do find it difficult to talk in a group and need the leader's help to make their points of view known. You may see them change their seating position, lean forward, wave their pencil etc., just before they want to speak. Look out for these indicators and take advantage by inviting them to speak.

Other members are naturally quiet, which does not mean that they are not contributing. They may be thinking and listening very hard but feel no need to contribute. You must check with these people from time to time that they are happy with the discussion. If you are very concerned, talk to them on their own during a break to check how they feel.

72

The third kind of quiet member is the 'enforced silence' person. This type of person may be contributing fully up to a certain point and then will suddenly 'switch off' and drop out of the debate. Something has happened to cause this behaviour. They may have had ideas dismissed several times by a more dominant person, or have been regularly interrupted whilst trying to contribute. Something may have been agreed by the group with which they have a serious problem and have not been allowed a fair hearing. Whatever the reason, it is important that you are alert to such changes. Start to encourage the member to contribute, and try to find out what has caused the drop in contribution.

The main requirement with all types of quiet members is to be alert to their non-contribution, encourage participation and check that there is not a problem. If there is no problem and they are comfortable with what is happening, they should not be forced to contribute for the sake of it.

Shutting out

With dominant members, the leader controls their contribution in a more assertive, but nevertheless polite, way. The discussion leader will need to interrupt politely and take control of the situation. This is called 'shutting out' ('That's an interesting point, Bob. I want to come back to that but first I'd like to ask Jill and Tony what they think').

Whilst being assertive, it is essential that you are not dismissive or patronizing in approach and that you acknowledge any contribution already made. If the relationship is healthy between the member and the facilitator a quiet word before the session, or indeed, over coffee, may help. You must, however, tackle dominant players because of their potentially negative effect on the quieter individuals.

Summarizing is a good way of interrupting. It acknowledges what is being said but at the same time allows you to regain control.

If the main session results in the same few people talking all the time – despite your best efforts – you must then consider how any syndicate teams should be selected. If the same mixture of dominant and quiet is reflected in syndicate groups, according to who is chosen for each team, the same problems will exist.

A better way to split the team is to place all the dominant members in one sub-group and all the quiet ones in the other. That way the quiet members will be placed together in an environment where they are more likely to contribute. The dominant member sub-group is guaranteed to be more lively, but this will provide an excellent medium for the facilitator to make them examine their own behaviours and the effect that they have on the quality of the discussion.

When handling both types of individual, however, you must stay neutral. Acknowledge all contributions as valid and do not take sides. The strong need protecting as much as the weak – even though at times it's from themselves!

As the group develops, the extent of these problems lessens. Both types of individual will have been given feedback on their behaviour and its impact on the group. The increased self-awareness, levels of openness and comfort with each other's natural styles all help to minimize any problems caused. One could almost argue that the only reason for having a facilitator at times is to control the poor behaviours of team members!

Warming up groups

Teambuilding can be perceived as a risky business by the individuals participating, particularly if they have no previous experience. Therefore, it is necessary at the start of any session to warm the group up in some way before undertaking the first serious piece of work. It could almost be likened to visiting friends, when you take your coat off and go through the pleasantries before you settle down to the real reason for the visit.

It is advisable, therefore, to incorporate within any design some sort of short activity after the first introduction to the day. Some options are outlined in the exercises section, but it is worth mentioning the point here as it is an important part of ensuring the effectiveness of the day. Sharing expectations and listing ground rules, both written on a flipchart are good methods, as is picture modelling (see Part III, 'Getting Started'). The key point about these methods is that they all involve individual physical activity. Getting members out of their seats, writing on flipchart paper and sharing their thoughts serves the following purposes:

- It forces all to participate.
- The physical nature of the activity can relieve possible tension.
- It provides early feedback to the facilitator and team leader as to the frame of mind of individuals (e.g. level of anxiousness, perceived importance, and energy for the session).

Whatever the warm-up exercise, keep it simple and fairly brief, say,

30–40 minutes. Also keep it relevant to the day's objectives – irrelevant 'games' could irritate some members.

Large and small groups

The size of the group you will work with is dictated by the natural workgroup size and the objectives and attendance as outlined earlier. There are a number of implications to consider when running sessions with particularly large groups or small groups of 3 or 4 members. Let us look at each in turn.

Large groups

Large groups consist of 8 or more members. Predictable difficulties here include the following:

- **Highly variable levels of individual contribution and openness in the main sessions**. It is easier for people to 'hide' and make minimum contributions and some members will find it harder to speak up in a large forum.
- **Increased difficulty handling a discussion with a large group**. Balancing contribution and gaining consensus, where necessary, can be very difficult. During the course of the discussion the percentage time allowed for each individual to have his or her say is naturally reduced.
- **Multiple syndicates or sub-groups, which require several (up to 4 or 5) presentations back to the whole group**. The time taken for presentations will eat away at the available time on the day and can produce too much of a conference-like feel to the session.
- **An excess of sweeping generalizations and vague statements**. Issues raised by members can either be so broad as to be unhelpful or so specific that they only interest a minority of the group. As some members may be reluctant to share personal thoughts, it is easy to gain an unbalanced perspective, biased by the loud and assertive members who may place too much emphasis on their own requirements. Watch out for this when the group size is a dozen or more people; in some such circumstances a team session can easily become a discontented, fragmented affair.

The following actions, some of which may need to be included at the design stage, may help to solve such problems:

- **Give syndicates different briefs so as to make best use of the group's resources**. This also avoids presentations back to the main group being repetitive. For example, if reviewing meeting effectiveness with four syndicates, have two of them look at the purpose and content of meetings, whilst the other two look at the process and behaviours in their meetings.
- **Once problems that need to be addressed have been identified, break the group into sub-groups to discuss and work on them**. The sub-groups can be chosen or the individuals allowed to choose which problem they want to work on, a groundrule being that each group must be roughly the same size. Sometimes, the sub-groups will present themselves naturally as a result of the issues raised.
- **Allow a decent amount of time for syndicate working, say, up to 4 hours, to allow quality work**. Short syndicates will produce short answers, often unconsidered, which can perpetuate generalizations.
- **Where sharing of personal feedback is planned, allow this in sub-groups with no presentation back to the main group**. Alternatively, you can ask them to share only outcomes that they feel appropriate and want the whole group to hear.
- **Control the main group discussions tightly**, keeping the group focused, and avoid side-tracking. Keep a flipchart handy to list any side issues raised that the group do not want to lose but which would side-track the session at that time. If necessary break the group into syndicates and run parallel discussions.
- **Challenge vague statements and ask for examples**. Challenge words and phrases like 'always', 'everyone', 'all the time' etc.
- **'Bring in' quiet members**. If testing for final agreement, go round every member of the group and get a positive response. *Do not* say 'Everyone agree?', wait ten seconds, and then assume that silence means 'yes'!
- **As a way of bringing a working session to a close, and at the same time, testing levels of commitment, consider asking each person to write down the main point learnt from the discussion**. Then have each individual quickly and succinctly call out their conclusions. If the group is not too big, list the responses on a flipchart.

Small groups

Small groups consist of 3 or 4 members. Predictable difficulties here include the following:

- **Difficulty in getting the group to talk with each other** *across the table rather than through the facilitator*. It can be a strange experience to have 'A' sharing a problem about 'B' by talking to you, the facilitator, when person 'B' is sitting next to them!
- **The temptation to keep the group together throughout the session and not use paired or individual working**. This can get very tiring if the team session lasts more than 3 to 4 hours. Some variation will certainly help keep up energy levels and concentration.
- **The team leader dominating and/or becoming the continual focus of the discussions**. How he or she behaves in small group sessions is important if open and equal discussion is to be achieved. (This also applies when the leader is working as a participant in a syndicate group.)

Some ideas that may help with these situations are as follows:

- **Confronting the group skilfully when they are not talking to each other**. In the example above, bring in 'B' and ask him or her directly to respond to 'A' (e.g. 'Sue's made a good point there, John, what's your view of it?').
- **As the facilitator, having introduced the subject for discussion – or posed a question to the group – stay quiet and do not be drawn back in**. If necessary, pull your chair away from the table and sit out of the group. Tell the group you are going to sit out and want them to discuss that particular issue to a conclusion. In some cases, consider leaving the room (discreetly!) for a short period.
- **Use paired working and individual working to bring variety into the day**. Have them leave the room to work in quiet corners of the hotel for half an hour. Make sure, as the facilitator, that you do not do all the writing on flipcharts. On occasions, give the pen to one individual and ask them to write instead.
- **Warn the team leader about the possible impact of his or her role and behaviour before the session** – but make sure that he or she is not perceived by the group as playing games. Make sure, when eliciting views around the table, that you do not start or finish with the team leader each time. Treat him or her as an equal member in any discussion.

Syndicate and buzz groups

Skilful use of syndicates, buzz groups or individual working prior

Table 2: Advantages and disadvantages of working formats

Format	Advantages	Disadvantages
Syndicates	– Time for considered responses – Different briefs for each group can allow better use of resources – Written outcomes for reference – Can be extended into problem-solving sessions	– Need extra rooms – Variable contributions can continue – Time consuming – Last syndicate to present back may find all their input already covered – Spreads facilitator resource thinly
Buzz groups	– Keeps energy up – Ensures participation by all – Quick input for group discussion	– Requires large main room – May produce superficial response
Individual working	– Quick – No special facilities needed – Ensures participation by all	– Possible reduction in creativity – Individuals work at different rates – difficult to judge when to call a stop

to a main group discussion, can go a long way to adding variety and ensuring effective use of time and resources.

Syndicates   The group is split into sub-groups of 3–6 individuals and given a brief to go away and complete. Usually, the minimum period is 30–40 minutes but they could work for up to 4 hours on an issue. The syndicates work in separate rooms and return when finished to present their deliberations formally in the main group.

Buzz groups   Small groups of 2 or 3 are asked a question and given anywhere from 5 to 15 minutes to review their thoughts. The groups stay in the main room, simply pulling their chairs together. They may often be made up of people seated next to each other, but not necessarily so. They take notes whilst sharing ideas, and presentation back to the main group is usually informal and done verbally, the facilitator possibly noting points on the flipchart during the presentation.

Individual working   Individuals are posed a question, asked to think (5–10 minutes) and to write down their answers, to be shared verbally later with the whole group.

Each method presents ways of breaking up a session, adding variety and raising or lowering energy levels (the latter applying to individual working when quiet reflection is requested). They can each be used as different ways of addressing the same issue (e.g. developing group objectives, reviewing learning to date, identifying characteristics of an effective team etc.), which is usually done at the design stage.

A list of the benefits and negatives of each format is given in Table 2. One particular difference between them is worthy of special consideration. This is the time taken by each, as follows:

- Syndicate working followed by discussion will take a minimum of 2 hours (45 minutes in syndicate, 30 minutes to present back and 1 hour discussion in the main group).
- Buzz group working followed by discussion will take from 45 minutes to 1 hour (15 minutes' buzz group working, 30–45 minutes' discussion).
- Individual working followed by discussion can take as little as 30 minutes (5 minutes' individual working, 25 minutes' discussion).

During a session, flexible use of these methods can allow you to catch up lost time. If, for example, on a day's session you are an hour behind in the morning and plan a 2-hour syndicate and discussion session in the afternoon, use of buzz groups instead of full syndicates will allow you to get back on track.

Whichever technique is used, you should consider the following points:

- **Keep the briefs clear and simple**. Complex briefs or ambiguous questions can cause confusion. Check that the group understand what you want them to consider and what outputs are needed (e.g. flipchart presentation, checklist, recommendations etc.).
- **Once buzz groups or syndicates have started work, get round to each and test their understanding** of the brief, to make sure they are working on the right question.
- **Consider carefully the selection of individuals for both buzz groups or syndicates**. (See 'Dominant and quiet members' above.) You may wish to choose buzz groups from individuals *not* sitting together to ensure physical movement and activity. It is suprising sometimes how helpful getting people physically to change places can be!
- **Make sure that the syndicate rooms are set up with pens, flipcharts etc. and that the rooms are unlocked *before* you break the group up**. Otherwise, you can lose 15 minutes just setting up the groups!
- **When listing outcomes of buzz groups and individual working, use *their* words and do not manipulate what they say by use of the pen**. If they do not like what you have written, cross it out and re-write it – do not argue the point.
- **When using syndicates, make sure you remember their primary purpose – to provide *initial* input to a discussion**. The final group discussion is the important session. Keep the balance of time right between syndicate work and main group discussion. The only exception to this is where the syndicate session itself is planned as a quality problem-solving discussion (e.g. 4 hours to prepare recommendations on a new meeting structure).
- **With large groups try to avoid a repetitive cycle of syndicate–present–discuss, syndicate–present–discuss etc**. It is tempting, but it will produce a 'conference' feel to any workshop, with only superficial debate.

In summary, flexible and skilful use of syndicates, buzz groups and individual working can add greatly to the quality of output at a team session, whilst adding variety to the day and keeping energy levels high.

Energy levels

Energy levels within the group are likely to vary during a team session. A good design with some, but not excessive, variety in patterns of work will do much to keep energy high. The obvious periods to watch are at the start (see 'Warming up groups' above) and after lunch. The first session after lunch is often called the 'graveyard shift', when natural tiredness sets in. Some precautions that you can take to help alleviate this are as follows:

- Light lunches!
- Activity-based sessions straight after lunch (e.g. syndicated work, picture modelling (see Part III, Exercise 3 etc.), rather than films or presentations.
- Restricting any inputs to approximately 20 minutes.
- Using tea breaks or introducing additional 10-minute breaks for fresh air (e.g. to break up a series of presentations).
- On 2–3 day sessions, planning in a 'leisure break' of a couple of hours straight after lunch. It can often be better to do this and work from 4.00–7.30 p.m. than work straight through the afternoon.
- Extending the 'lunch hour' by planning in individual working. For example, give the group 2 hours to take lunch *and* individually complete a questionnaire. That way they can plan their own time, get some fresh air, work in their own room etc.

Be aware of the energy level of the group and do not plough on regardless. A drop in energy level may be due to general tiredness through concentration, the oppressive nature of the room or the presence of a problem with the issues being debated. If it is the last of these problems, it may be necessary to halt the session and get the group to review how it is feeling and what they want to do (see 'Hidden agendas' above). This may expose the issue and result in a replanning of the day and the original objectives.

The golden rule is to be flexible. Do not slavishly pursue an initial design that is not working! The essence of facilitating a teambuilding session is to guide and help the group on its own voyage of discovery.

The secret lies in creating an environment which, on the one hand, encourages openness and risk taking whilst, on the other, does not appear clumsy or overly threatening to those involved. A

carefully thought through design, based on an initial diagnosis, creates the platform to build on, but, as the content described above shows, the unpredictability of human interaction ensures that teambuilding is never a simple matter of processing teams through structured exercises!

The compensating factor is your skill as a facilitator in handling unplanned (though not necessarily unpredictable) behaviours and in adapting to changing situations during the session – but then that is half the fun of teambuilding! In selecting what to do when your session meets difficulties, a final piece of advice worth remembering is that *it is better to do nothing than to do the wrong thing*. If you are really not sure what to do, sit back, observe and collect more data about what is happening. If the focus is on you at the time, for example, you are handling a discussion – suggest a break and create time to think.

Facilitating is a skill in its own right and whilst it is not possible within the scope of this book to do the subject full justice, the suggestions above should help ensure you avoid the obvious pitfalls.

4 | Follow-up

The format of the follow-up depends in part on whether the team session was planned as a single event or the first of a series of sessions. However, the three essential areas to think about are as follows:

- Action plans and future sessions.
- Writing up the outcomes.
- Follow-up with individuals.

Action plans

If the session was one of a series, the manager will probably already have agreed a number of future dates with the team. If not, then this needs to be done to avoid slippage and allow any off-site locations to be booked.

During the session itself a number of action requirements will have been developed that will need to be written up and circulated to all team members. The leader must also decide how he or she will review progress against the actions agreed to ensure that they happen – a vital point to note. It is very easy for these requirements to be lost in the ensuing day-to-day activities – more so if the group is at an early stage of development.

There is no need for extensive diagnosis before each session if the session is one of a series of, say, bi-monthly sessions. You will gain sufficient 'live' data from each session to gauge the current health of the group. This is even more the case if you are working with members of the group in between sessions. However, if the next session is 6 months or more away, some form of diagnosis is advisable since much may have happened during the intervening period. Again, though, this may be done simply via a quick questionnaire with a few open questions (see Part III, Exercise 1, Document 1.3), to be returned to you before the workshop is planned.

Writing up the outcomes

Writing up the various flipcharts produced during the first session is a matter of choice. It can often be worthwhile to have summarized any conclusions, such as what the team does well or not so well, to use in the future as a benchmark against which to measure progress. Slavishly typing up every flipchart can be a chore, however, and is not always necessary. The more that is typed, the less likely it will be read again in the future! It is generally easy to pick out the few charts that are worth keeping, dependent on the subject matter covered on the day.

Follow-up with individuals

If you are working with the group on an ongoing basis, time permitting, it can be extremely valuable to follow up informally with each team member within a couple of weeks of the session. Test their reaction and comfort level with the session (Have they any concerns? Did they learn from the session? etc.). Following up individually will sometimes provide you with a unique opportunity to continue the teambuilding process – not all the teambuilding is done with the group as a whole! If your relationship is sound with each member the timing may be just right for, and the person highly receptive to, further feedback on his or her behaviours or discussion of his or her problems with the team. As a minimum you *must* follow up with the team leader and review the effectiveness of the workshop. He or she is your client!

Part III—Teambuilding tools and techniques

Introduction

Part III contains fourteen sets of activities, all designed to be used within teambuilding programmes. The activities cover the following three main areas:

- Diagnosis   Exercise 1
- Getting started   Exercises 2–4
- Improving team effectiveness   Exercises 5–14

Exercise 1 provides tools that can be used to diagnose the effectiveness of a team either at the start or during an ongoing teambuilding programme. The activities suggested cover the use of both questionnaire and interview techniques. Exercises 2–4 are simple activities that can be used at the start of a teambuilding session to warm up the group and achieve early participation by all. Exercises 5–14 include a miscellany of tools and techniques that can be used to tackle typical team issues, from goal clarity through to meetings effectiveness and decision-making processes.

Each exercise has been designed as a stand-alone module to be run separately or in combination with other exercises during a longer programme. Specific objectives are given for each exercise, and advice on when and how to use it. Correctly judging the current stage of the group's development and its specific needs, and matching this with an appropriate activity, is very necessary if maximum benefit is to be gained from the use of an activity. To that end the activities have been designed with the various stages of group development in mind (see Part I, Chapter 1, 'How does a group develop?').

Where specific advice is given on the timing of an activity, it is wise to follow such guidance. A wrongly timed activity will at best appear clumsy to the group and at worst could damage the teambuilding process. The group is most vulnerable to this fault as it moves through the 'storming' stage of its development.

All the activities have been used extensively with actual work teams. As far as possible, advice is given on: how the activity runs in practice; predictable outcomes; and potential difficulties and how to either pre-empt or handle them. Clearly, all eventualities cannot be covered, as each group is unique. It is hoped, however, that by sharing the benefit of actual experiences some surprises will be averted.

In the section on 'Exercise selection' in Part II, Chapter 2, a number of points were made about the use of exercises. One or two are probably worth re-emphasizing as follows:

- Each activity is only a means to an end. What is important is the purpose of each session. The tool or technique is only the 'key to the door'. Use the activities to create the environment for discussion, and if the plan is not working, be prepared to change it.
- When combining activities within a programme or a 2–3 day event, link the activities, starting with broader issues before moving on to activities requiring specific personal feedback. Use the hierarchy of 'goals', 'roles', 'processes' and 'relationships' as a framework to help determine the order in which you work on the team issues (see 'What are the main problems encountered by teams?' in Part I, Chapter 1).
- Do not be too ambitious with regard to how much you will be able to cover in a given time. Keep it simple and use the guidelines on time in each activity liberally. Be prepared to drop or modify an activity on the day.

The activities have been written to cover the typical range of issues that are likely to arise when working with a group. They have also been chosen to illustrate the use of a range of techniques (syndicates, buzz groups etc.). They are not definitive and can be modified if that is helpful. When designing and running teambuilding programmes always feel free to change and adapt the ideas to suit your own needs, for example, by modifying the questions or including short tutorials or skills building sessions when you feel they are needed.

Finally, remember there is no single correct way to design a teambuilding programme. There is no formula of activities that will convert a group into a perfect team! The activities represent a 'palette' of ideas and their effectiveness depends on your skill as a facilitator in helping the group to find their own way towards improved performances. Good luck . . .

In the exercises which follow, the handout sheets for group participants are indicated by the handout symbol in the top left-hand margin on each page.

List of exercises

1—Diagnosis

2—Getting started

3—Improving team effectiveness

1 | Diagnosis

Good diagnosis of a team's current effectiveness is a necessary precursor to effective programme design. Without it any design will be based on guesswork and assumption and at best may result in a clumsily run session. It is also important that the facilitator has forewarning of any potential tensions and difficulties which could arise during the day.

The following section outlines two basic techniques of data collection: interviews and questionnaire approaches. The ground covered by both methods is similar but, time permitting, interviews will provide more qualitative data. Through discussion the facilitator will be able to assess the strength of feelings and receptiveness to change of each team member.

Clarifying the need

Purpose

- To provide initial data to identify the needs with regard to teambuilding or to review progress being made during a teambuilding programme.

Application

- This exercise can be carried out by the team leader or by a facilitator to establish the current effectiveness of the team. It forms a critical part of planning a teambuilding programme or individual team session.
- The tools provided below cover diagnosis by one-to-one interviews or via a questionnaire.
- Both the Interview Checklist (Document 1.1) and the Team Effectiveness Questionnaire (Document 1.2) are aimed at an initial, full diagnosis before a programme is started.
- The Team Development Questionnaire (Document 1.3) is planned for use during an ongoing programme, to check progress. If an interview process is preferred at this stage, the questions within the questionnaire can be used as a basis for the interview.
- The questionnaires can be used either named or anonymously.

Time required

Variable   2–8 hours dependent on method used.

Materials needed

- Interview Checklist (Document 1.1).
- Team Effectiveness Questionnaire (Document 1.2) (1 per team member).
- Team Development Questionnaire (Document 1.3) (1 per team member).

Process

The tools below provide for data collection by either one-to-one interviews with team members or a questionnaire completed individually and returned to the sender for analysis. For a fuller discussion on the merits of each technique and which to use, see Part II, Chapter 1, 'Diagnosis'. Also included is guidance for a manager on whether to conduct the exercise personally or to use a facilitator.

Interview Checklist (Document 1.1)

Prior to conducting any interviews, the team leader needs to explain the purpose of the exercise to the group and, if not already done, introduce his or her intentions regarding teambuilding. If a facilitator is used, they will also need to be introduced to the group.

As with any data collection exercise, the leader or facilitator needs to reassure the group as to how the data will be analysed and used. If a facilitator is employed it is normal practice that the data he or she shares with the team leader is of a *general* nature only – even though the interviews will elicit quite personal views.

The list of pointers below provides a framework for the interview which will take approximately 1 hour for each team member. Use the Interview Checklist as a guide only and allow the conversation to flow freely. Used too rigidly, like a tick sheet, it will greatly restrict conversation. The following are some pointers to remember whilst conducting the interview:

- Keep the session as informal as possible.
- Introduce the session, reaffirming its purpose, what is required, and what will happen to the data given.
- Use open questions and encourage the other person to talk. Follow up general answers with probing questions (e.g. 'Can you explain further?', 'What exactly do you mean?', 'What exactly happened?' etc.).
- Make sure you avoid leading questions which imply the answer (e.g. 'I take it that team meetings could be significantly improved?').
- Stay neutral and try to avoid information gathered from others influencing your questions. It is easy after three or four interviews to make an evaluation – for example, that objectives are not understood – and to start asking closed questions to confirm your judgement.
- Start by asking questions about non-threatening areas of team performance, such as objectives. Leave questions about personal feelings and relationships until later on in the

interview, when the individual starts to feel more comfortable. The Interview Checklist questions have been ordered with this in mind.

- To some extent allow the interviewee to talk about subjects in the order he or she most wants to share them. In other words if the interviewee is particularly concerned about a team issue and raises it early in the session before you had intended to cover it, talk about it then rather than keep saying 'We'll come back to that'. Simply make sure that by the end of the interview you have covered all the main areas.
- Be sensitive to the interviewee's feelings and needs – especially if the group is at an early stage of development. Probe, but do not force, members to share personal views if they are not comfortable. How open they are will provide a real measure of the team's current climate.
- Close the interview by reaffirming how you will use the data and what the individual can expect to happen next.
- A final word of caution – for a facilitator, conducting the interviews provides an opportunity to gain the team's confidence but also to create distrust and discomfort. If the interview is conducted clumsily or if data is not treated confidentially, the facilitator's ability to work with the team may be severely diminished.

Team Effectiveness Questionnaire (Document 1.2)

Again, the team leader must explain the purpose of the exercise to the group and introduce his or her intentions regarding team-building. This can be done at one of the team's normal meetings, and the questionnaire should be issued at the same time. However, if the questionnaire is mailed to team members, make sure a covering letter is included from the team leader explaining its purpose and how the data is to be used.

The questionnaire should be given out at least 2–3 weeks before the session with a deadline set for its return. Always allow some time to chase up late replies. The recipient can be asked to complete it anonymously if that is felt appropriate, or to post a copy direct to the facilitator. Ideally, though, encourage individuals to be open and sign the form, but not if you think it will seriously restrict openness.

Once collected, analyse the data to identify the main themes and issues for sharing with the team leader. Make sure that in sharing the data no individuals are inadvertently identified – unless that has already been agreed with the team.

The questionnaire will take individuals a maximum of 40

minutes to complete. If they spend any longer on it, it is unlikely to yield better data, so encourage them not to over-deliberate.

Team Development Questionnaire (Document 1.3)

This is a much simpler questionnaire for use during an ongoing programme. Ideally it should be used 4–6 months into any teambuilding programme to reassess progress. For example, if the programme has started with a couple of early sessions in months 1 and 2, and with a planned session in month 6, the questionnaire is an ideal way to collect data before the third session.

As with the Team Effectiveness Questionnaire it should be distributed 2–3 weeks before the session for return and use in planning the session. Individuals should be allowed 30–45 minutes to complete it. As an alternative, the questions can be used as a simple interviewing format. If so, allow 45 minutes to 1 hour for each interview.

Notes

- Whilst data collection is an important part of teambuilding, if a programme is constructed which involves, say, monthly sessions for 6 months, it is not necessary to collect data before each session. At such frequencies each session itself provides data on the progress of the group, particularly if at some of the sessions a formal review is conducted.
- If tools like the Team Development Questionnaire are given out too frequently, they are likely to irritate and provide poor data. Having identified strengths and areas for improvement, the group members should be allowed time to work together before formal data collection exercises are conducted again.
- If the team is well established and regularly reviewing its own progress, there is less need for formal data collection in order to design an effective session. However, if a facilitator is brought back into the group after 6 months or more, they will be out of touch. In this case, a formal data collection will help the facilitator 'tune in' to the group's stage of development.

Variation

- Whilst the aim of these tools is to collect data to establish the need for teambuilding and to plan an appropriate programme, the data collected could also be used as a starting point for discussion in a team session in much the same way as the questionnaires in Exercise 7.

Interview Checklist

Team purpose and objectives

- To what extent do you feel the group needs to work as a team?
- How would you describe the primary purpose of the team?
- What do you see as the team's main objectives for the next 12 months?
- What are the priorities?
- How are objectives developed and agreed? How do you feel about the process?
- How committed are individuals in the team to the team's objectives?
- How does the team review its objectives? What actions are taken if objectives are not being achieved?

Role clarity

- How clear are you about your own role and objectives?
- How clear are others about your role and objectives?
- How clear are you about others' roles and objectives?
- What help do you need from the team to achieve your objectives? Do you get it?
- How do you know if you are seen to be performing well or badly – by the leader and by the team?

Communication

- How do you view communications across the team and between the team and the leader?
- How open are individuals with their views?
- To what extent do individuals listen to each other and seek feedback?
- How would you describe the overall atmosphere in the team?

Reproduced from *Building a Better Team*,
by Peter Moxon, Gower, Aldershot, 1993.

Decision making

- How are decisions made within the team?
- How do you view the general quality of decisions made?
- To what extent do you and others feel involved and committed to decisions made?
- To what extent do you feel you can personally influence decisions?

Team meetings

- How effective are the team meetings?
- What is the general level of participation by team members?
- What do you like/dislike about the meetings?
- Do you get what you need from the meetings?
- How do team members behave within the meetings? In what way does this help/hinder the meetings?

Relationships within the team

- What are relationships like within the team?
- What are relationships like between the leader and the team?
- If conflicts arise, what generally happens?
- How do team members behave towards each other?

Relationships with others

- What are the relationships like with other outside areas that the team deals with?
- What are the problem areas, if any, and why?

Leadership style

- How would you describe the leader's style and approach?
- How comfortable is the team with his/her approach?
- What do you like the leader to do more of and less of in his/her dealings with the team?

Reproduced from *Building a Better Team*,
by Peter Moxon, Gower, Aldershot, 1993.

Individual contribution

– How comfortable do you feel with your own contribution to the team?
– What do you believe you bring to the team?
– What do you most want from working in the team?
– What are your biggest frustrations, working in the team?

Overall team effectiveness

– How would you summarize the team's strengths?
– How would you summarize the team's main areas for improvement?
– What one or two things, if improved, would have the most impact on the team's effectiveness and performance?

Teambuilding programme

– How do you feel about attending a teambuilding session?
– What do you most want to get out of it?
– What worries, if any, do you have?
– How important do you feel the session is?

Reproduced from *Building a Better Team*,
by Peter Moxon, Gower, Aldershot, 1993.

Team Effectiveness Questionnaire

Date: _____

Name: _____

Instructions

This questionnaire is a means of assessing the current effectiveness of the team, as seen by individual team members.

The questionnaire identifies ten separate factors that cover the behaviours of effective and ineffective teams. For each factor there are short paragraphs describing the two ends of the spectrum. For each factor consider the two paragraphs and circle a score that represents whereabouts on the scale you view the team's *current* behaviours.

Please be honest in your replies. There are no right or wrong answers. The questionnaire is entirely subjective in reflecting your personal views and will provide a 'snapshot' of how you see the current situation with regard to the team's effectiveness.

Please complete the questionnaire and return a copy to ………
by ………………………… Retain a copy for yourself and bring it to the workshop.

Reproduced from *Building a Better Team*,
by Peter Moxon, Gower, Aldershot, 1993.

Questionnaire

For each factor please consider both paragraphs. Then circle the score for each factor that represents whereabouts on the scale you view the team's current behaviours.

1) Atmosphere

The 'atmosphere', which can be sensed in a few minutes of observation, tends to be informal, comfortable, relaxed. There are no obvious tensions. It is a working atmosphere in which people are involved and interested. There are no signs of boredom.

1 2 3 4 5 6 7

The 'atmosphere' is likely to reflect either indifference and boredom (e.g. people whispering to each other or carrying on side conversations, individuals who are obviously not involved), or tension (e.g. undercurrents of hostility and antagonism, stiffness and undue formality). The group is not challenged by its task or genuinely involved in it.

2) Group objectives

The task or the objective of the group is well understood and accepted by the members. There will have been free discussion of the objective at some point until it was formulated in such a way that the members of the group could commit themselves to it. Objectives are regularly reviewed and their achievement used as a measure of the group's success.

1 2 3 4 5 6 7

It is difficult to understand what the group task is or what its objectives are. These may have been stated by the chairman initially, but there is no evidence that the group either understands or accepts a common objective. It is usually evident that different people have different, personal objectives which they are attempting to achieve in the group. These are often in conflict with each other and with the group's task.

3) Communications

There is a lot of discussion in which virtually everyone participates, but it remains pertinent to the task of the group. If the discussion gets off the subject, someone will quickly bring it back into line. Individuals build on each other's ideas.

Team members listen to each other. The discussion does not have the quality of jumping from one idea to another unrelated one. Every idea is given a hearing. People do not appear to be afraid of being foolish by putting forth a creative thought even if it seems fairly extreme.

1 2 3 4 5 6 7

A few people tend to dominate the discussion. Often their contributions are off the point. Little is done by anyone to keep the group clearly on the track. Issues are overworked and there is little attention to timekeeping.

People do not really listen to each other. Ideas are ignored and overridden. The discussion jumps around with little coherence or purpose. There is talking for effect – people make speeches which are intended to impress rather than being relevant to the task at hand. Individuals leave team meetings not having expressed ideas or feelings.

4) Handling of conflict

There is disagreement but the group is comfortable handling conflict. Disagreements are not suppressed or overridden. They are viewed as expressions of genuine difference of opinion. The reasons are carefully examined, and the group seeks to resolve them rather than to dominate the dissenter. When disagreements cannot be resolved, the group can live with them, accepting them but not permitting them to block its efforts. Action may be deferred to permit further study of an issue.

1 2 3 4 5 6 7

Disagreements are not dealt with effectively by the group. They may be suppressed by the leader to avoid conflict or they may result in heated argument, the consequence of which is domination by one sub-group over another. Resolution may often be by voting leaving some individuals uncommitted. In general only the more dominant members get their ideas considered because the quieter people tend either to stay silent altogether, give up after ineffectual attempts to be heard or accede to preserve the peace or to get on with the task.

104

Reproduced from *Building a Better Team*,
by Peter Moxon, Gower, Aldershot, 1993.

5) Decision making

Most decisions are reached by an easy consensus in which it is clear that everybody is in general agreement and willing to go along. There is little tendency for individuals who oppose the action to keep their opposition private and thus let an apparent consensus mask real disagreement.

Formal voting is at a minimum; the group does not accept a simple majority as a proper basis for action. Individuals are clear as to their own authority levels with respect to the leader.

1 2 3 4 5 6 7

Actions are often taken prematurely before the real issues are either examined or resolved. There will be much grousing after the meeting by people who disliked a decision but failed to speak up about it in the meeting itself.

A simple majority is considered sufficient for action, and the minority is expected to go along, leaving individuals or minorities uncommitted to the decisions. The leader will often use his/her position to force decisions through.

6) Criticism

Criticism is frequent, frank and relatively comfortable. There is little evidence of personal attack, either openly or in a hidden fashion. The criticism is constructive and oriented toward removing obstacles that face the group and are preventing the group from getting the job done.

1 2 3 4 5 6 7

Criticism may be present, but it is embarrassing and tension producing. It often appears to involve personal hostility, and team members are uncomfortable with this. Criticism of ideas tends to be destructive. Individuals are quick to evaluate others' proposals, seeing only the negatives. There is little building on others' contributions.

7) Expression of personal feelings

People are free in expressing their feelings as well as their ideas, both on the problem and on the group's operation. There are few 'hidden agendas'. Dialogue is open and honest with individuals prepared to accept feedback. There is a high level of trust within the group.

1 2 3 4 5 6 7

Personal feelings are hidden rather than being out in the open. Individuals are not prepared to take any risks. The general attitude of the group is that these are inappropriate for discussion or would be destructive if brought out on the table.

105

Reproduced from *Building a Better Team*, by Peter Moxon, Gower, Aldershot, 1993.

8) Task achievement

Clear action plans are agreed to progress issues. Assigned responsibilities are unambiguous. There is a high level of commitment by all to actions agreed and actions are always followed through and reviewed. The group regularly reviews performance against objectives and acts to ensure success.

1 2 3 4 5 6 7

Action decisions tend to be unclear – no one really knows who is going to do what. Even when assignments of responsibility are made, there is often considerable doubt as to whether they will be carried out. There is minimal follow-up to agreed actions and variable commitment. Performance is rarely reviewed. Poor performance is rationalized.

9) Leadership

The leader does not dominate, nor, on the contrary, does the group defer unduly to him/her. Leadership shifts around the group from time to time, depending on the circumstances. There is little evidence of a struggle for power as the group operates. The issue is not who controls but how to get the job done.

1 2 3 4 5 6 7

The leadership remains clearly with the team leader. He/she will either dominate and control the group, sanctioning or taking all important decisions, or abdicate the leadership role. When the latter is the case the group does not 'fill the gap' but instead remains leaderless.

10) Review of team processes

The group is conscious about its own operations. Frequently, it will stop to examine how well it is doing or what may be interfering with its operations. The problem may be a matter of procedure, or it may be an individual whose behaviour is interfering with the accomplishment of the group's objectives. Whatever it is, there is open discussion until a solution is found.

1 2 3 4 5 6 7

The group tends to avoid discussion on the effectiveness of its own operation. There is often much discussion outside team meetings of what was wrong and why, but these matters are seldom brought up and considered within the meeting itself for resolution.

List other comments on a separate sheet if necessary.

106

Reproduced from *Building a Better Team*,
by Peter Moxon, Gower, Aldershot, 1993.

Document 1.3 | Team Development Questionnaire

Date: _____

Name: _____

Instructions

As part of the preparation for our next teambuilding session, please complete the following questionnaire. Its purpose is to:

- Give you an opportunity individually to review our progress before the meeting; and

- Provide data to allow us to plan the meeting to ensure we make the best use of time together.

Please complete the questionnaire and return a copy to ………
by ……………… Retain a copy for yourself and bring it along to the session.

Questionnaire

Q1. What have been the team's successes and failures (in terms of results) since our last session?

Q2. How has our teamworking developed since the last session?

    a) Where have we improved?

    b) Where have we slipped/not improved?

Q3. What changes are needed to further improve the group's effectiveness? Please prioritize your list and highlight the top three areas for attention.

Reproduced from *Building a Better Team*,
by Peter Moxon, Gower, Aldershot, 1993.

Q4. What do you view as the main business challenges and the main areas of vulnerability over the next 18 months?

a)   For the team's areas of responsibility?

b)   For your own area of responsibility?

Q5. What frustrates you most at present in achieving your own objectives? What help do you most want from the group?

Q6. What would you most want to gain from our next team-building session?

Reproduced from *Building a Better Team*,
by Peter Moxon, Gower, Aldershot, 1993.

2 | Getting started

One of the hardest parts of a teambuilding session is getting the team relaxed and talking and setting a constructive tone to the day. The sooner this is achieved the more productive will be the outcome.

The exercises in this next session offer some simple techniques to get the group working very early on in that day, sharing what they want to get out of the day or, in the case of a new team, introducing each other.

With a group that is known to have tensions and problems between individuals, agreeing some basic ground rules of how each needs to behave during the session is particularly useful. Included within the activities is a simple method for achieving this. Done at the start of the day it affords the facilitator the opportunity to emphasize any unhelpful behaviour, particularly pertinent to the group he or she is working with, for example, poor listening, riding hobby-horse or dominant team members not allowing others to contribute. Once listed the ground rules can be used as a reference point if the group behaviour slips as the day progresses.

**Exercise
2**

What do individuals
want out of the
session?

Expectations and ground rules

Purpose

- To start the team session and to have everyone contributing.
- To understand what each team member wants from the session.
- To agree some ground rules for team operation during the day.

Application

- This exercise can be used by any group, irrespective of its stage of development. It is particularly important if the group is in the storming stage. A set of ground rules will help in the handling of any serious conflict during the day.
- It provides a good early indicator of the level of energy or apprehension with regard to the day ahead.
- It is generally used at the start of a team session following the introduction.

Time required

Total time		Approximately 45 minutes
Part I	Expectations	25 minutes
Part II	Ground rules	20 minutes

Materials needed

- Flipchart and pens.
- Masking tape.

Process

After stating the day's objectives, introduce the exercise by explaining the importance (a) for members to reveal and share what it is they want from the day, and (b) for the group to develop a set of ground rules covering how they will work together during the day, so that they make best use of the time.

Part I   Expectations

Give out a sheet of flipchart paper and a pen to each group member and ask them to list what they personally want to gain from the day. Allow 10 minutes for this part and ask members to post the flipcharts on the walls of the room. Ask each person in turn to talk through their flipchart. It will be necessary to probe some individuals to be more specific and not simply to repeat the objectives for the day. The aim is to have them talking and to understand their personal emphasis.

Once all have had a chance to share their views, summarize the main themes that have been presented. Be honest with individuals if you can see that a particular, often very specific, expectation is unlikely to be met, due, for example, to time constraints. Explain that it is their responsibility to ensure that their objectives are met during the day, and that you will revisit them at the end of the day to see how they have done.

At this stage it is essential not to work any of the issues raised and to keep the pace of the exercise going – particularly if there are more than 6 or 7 members in the group.

Part II   Ground rules

Next, divide the group into pairs and ask each pair to list down any key ground rules that the group must abide by in order to ensure that the day is productive. You may have to illustrate one or two examples. Allow 10 minutes for this.

Have individuals call out the ground rules and list them on a flipchart. Some typical examples would be as follows:

- Listening actively.
- No interrupting.
- All participate.
- Say what you mean – be honest.
- Constructive criticism.
- If you don't agree, say so.
- Be open.
- If you don't understand, ask questions.
- No hobby horses.
- Stay on track.
- Arrive back from syndicates/coffee on time.

Reinforce any of the ground rules that you know, from your knowledge of the group, will be difficult for them to follow (e.g. hobby horses). You may wish also to elaborate on one or two of the most significant rules (e.g. listening). You could do this by asking the member who introduced the rule what he or she meant by it or how it would be apparent in practice.

Taking a little time over the words is particularly useful with a group whose meeting behaviours are poor.

Post the flipchart and explain that you will be using this during the day, and that from time to time may ask the group to review how they are doing against the checklist of ground rules.

Notes

- You have to keep this exercise short (maximum 45 minutes), but without being superficial. With a large group of over 8 people, split them into buzz groups and have them work on both briefs at the same time. Give them 20 minutes and then have them present a flipchart showing their sub-group's expectations for the day. You could also ask them to collate their ground rules, to call them out when asked, or similarly, to present them on a flipchart.
- If a series of team sessions are to be run, the ground rules can be used at each session and need not be reworked. (Some groups may even decide to use them at their meetings back on-site.)
- Do not be surprised with a new group if their expectations are very superficial. It may be that they are not used to being asked the question or genuinely do not know what to expect.

One picture is worth
a thousand words

Picture modelling

Purpose

- To start the team session and have everyone contributing.
- To raise the energy level or remove some of the possible tensions.

Application

- This exercise can be used with a group at any stage. With a group in the storming stage, there may be some resistance from members who view it as trivial.
- It can be used at the start of a teambuilding session or during the session to raise energy levels (e.g. directly after lunch).
- It can provide a powerful way of uncovering hidden views and messages.

Time required

Total time		20–30 minutes
Part I	Individual working	10–15 minutes
Part II	Sharing	15 minutes

Materials needed

- Flipchart paper and pens.
- Masking tape.

Process

Part I

This is a very quick, high energy exercise. Explain to the group that you want each member to draw a picture that illustrates in both words (on the chart) and pictures how they personally 'see' the group. Ask them to work quickly and be creative, as one aim of the exercise is to have some fun. Spread the group out around the room. Allow 10 minutes (15 minutes maximum) for this part.

Part II

Either have each member keep their 'picture' and not share it until you ask, or have them post them on the wall. Go around the group and ask them to explain their picture to the group. Probe with the odd question yourself and ask the group if they have any questions.

The aim is to conduct the exercise quickly but do not be surprised if some very telling comments about the group come out – for example, members' views on cliques or parochialism within the group or how the group relates to other teams within the organization.

With a new group, the pictures may be very simple. With a group which is functioning poorly, this may well be vividly portrayed in their pictures with a surprising commonality of view. In this way, the exercise can provide a good way of indirectly bringing forward significant issues for discussion. If this happens, you will have to choose whether to deal with those issues immediately whilst the energy level is high or to return to them later on in the teambuilding session.

Notes

- With a large group (8 or over) you may need to split them into buzz groups and have each sub-group produce a picture.
- You must emphasize *words* and pictures in the brief. The less creative members may struggle with drawing and a few key words on a chart can say just as much.

Variations

- There are endless variations on this technique which can be used to obtain a 'snapshot' of a team's views on a variety of subjects, for example:

    How they are viewed by other areas.
    How they manage change.
    How they conduct their meetings.
    How they see themselves now, and how they wish to see themselves in 6 months' time.

How they see each other.
How they manage.

Any one of these subjects could prove a non-threatening route into sharing hidden agendas and personal perspectives. As such, the exercise does not necessarily need to be 'planned into' the day but can be used on the spur of the moment to great effect.

Paired interviews

Purpose

- To start the team session and get everyone contributing.
- To introduce members who do not know each other.

Application

- This is particularly useful with a new group, such as a taskforce or project team brought together for the first time.

Time required

Total time   1 hour
Part I   30 minutes
Part II   30 minutes

Materials needed

- Writing pads and pens.
- Safety pins.
- Flipchart and pens.

Process

Part I

Divide the group into pairs or trios. Keep members who do know each other apart. Explain that the purpose of the exercise is to learn about each other and to start sharing views with each other.

Inform them that they have 20 minutes in pairs (or 30 minutes if trios) for this part of the exercise, during which time you want them to interview each other. Tell them there are three areas that you want them to explore about their partners – the three **P**'s!:

- **Person:**   home background/hobbies/likes and dislikes etc.
- **Profession:** their current job responsibilities/career history and experience.
- **Purpose:**   what they expect to gain from being in the project team and what are some of their hopes and fears.

Ask them to find out a few facts about each of the three areas and explain that you want them to introduce their partner to the group at the end of the 20 minutes.

You emphasize that each person should take only a half (or a third) of the time, and that they will need to be careful that the second person is not left with only 2–3 minutes in which to do their full interview! (Invariably the 20 minutes will over-run, so plan for it! Once individuals start talking about themselves, it is hard to stop them!)

Part II

At the end of Part I, go round the group and have each of the members stand up and introduce his or her partner. For each person make a few notes on the flipchart of his or her 'purpose' statements. This will serve as a useful summary. Probe and test for clarification if necessary. Ask the group if they have any questions. Keep the pace up and do not allow the presentations to drag on.

Notes

With a large group (8 or more) there is a danger that the initial energy levels raised whilst interviewing will start to be lost if there are many presentations. For such groups, form buzz groups of 4 people, allow 30 minutes working in the group and then have one person from each group introduce the individuals in their buzz group and their group's expectations. Get each buzz group to write their 'purpose' statements on a flipchart before presenting.

Variations

- A more active variation of this exercise is to have each member answer the three **P**'s about him- or herself and write the facts on a flipchart along with his or her name. Allow 10 minutes for this.

  Have each member fix the chart to his or her front. They then have to walk around the room, introduce themselves to as many people in the room as possible, and find out about the people they meet. Allow 20 minutes for this.

Needless to say, this variation requires a fairly large room, but it is a very good way of relieving any initial tensions. Also, in a large group not everyone will have a chance to 'meet'. In that case, once the exercise is complete, give each member the task of getting to know those they have not met by the end of the first day. They can do this over coffee, lunch etc.

3 | Improving team effectiveness

This final group of exercises comprises the bulk of the activities on which programmes can be based. A wide variety of activities is included exemplifying different techniques such as individual presentation, group discussion, and completion of questionnaires. They encompass the most common issues experienced by teams, for example, poor meetings, unclear roles and decision-making processes, individual behaviour, conflicting goals or priorities etc.

In both content and style the exercises provide a tapestry of tools and techniques which can easily be modified to suit particular situations and groups. Indeed this is encouraged and many of the exercises contain possible variations on their use. To that end it is intended that the activities act merely as a template that can be tailored within a particular design.

Successes and failures

Why is it that in some
situations the team
perform well and
other times they
don't?

Purpose

- To increase self-awareness of the team's natural strengths and weaknesses in the way they work.
- To identify conditions and factors that will help ensure success and minimize failure.

Application

- This can be used at any stage during a group's development. It is particularly good at raising self-awareness of what the group does naturally (e.g. responding to a crisis, ensuring clear responsibility etc.).
- It will help the group predict when they are vulnerable to possible failure. For example, it may prove necessary in a group that a single member is always nominated to champion a particular initiative to ensure deadlines are met.
- It also helps a group develop a knowledge of what success looks like to each person in the team.

Time required

Total time		2 hours
Part I	Syndicates	40 minutes
Part II	Presentation	20 minutes
Part III	Discussion and action planning	1 hour

Materials needed

  – Flipchart and pens.

Process

Part I

Introduce the exercise by explaining to the group that you want them to look at how they operate as a group and what conditions help to make them successful.

Ask the group to reflect back over 6–12 months and think of the 'successes' they feel they have had – results achieved that they feel particularly pleased with.

Have them call out their thoughts and list them on a flipchart headed 'Successes'. Repeat the process with a second chart headed 'Failures or disappointments'. On this, list the results or actions that they considered did not work or with which they were disappointed.

You will find that members in the group may differ in their views of whether a specific action or result was a success or a failure. For example, the introduction of a new appraisal system – one person may feel it went well, another badly. Or both may agree that one aspect went well (e.g. initial communication) and the rest badly.

If quick agreement is forthcoming on what was good and what was bad, list the various aspects on the relevant chart. If you cannot reach agreement on an issue, list it on both charts and put a question mark beside it. Explain that the group will have a chance to debate their conclusions more fully in the next part of the exercise. Do not allow the group to debate the issues at this stage – the aim is simply to generate two basic lists for them to do further work on.

Part II

Split the group into two syndicates. Give each syndicate one of the sets of flipcharts – *either* successes or failures. Brief both groups to discuss their own list further. Ask them to identify why a particular issue was successful or otherwise. What conditions made this so? What did they do as a group to contribute to its success or failure?

Following their discussion, ask them to list the common factors that contributed to success or failure on each aspect, and to prepare a short presentation of their conclusions. Stress that it is *only* their conclusions that you want them to share, with a few examples to support them.

123

Factors which might appear on the lists are as follows:

- A clear plan.
- Some members were not committed.
- It was not seen at the time as a very important issue.
- It was a crisis and they had to respond.
- A deadline had been agreed.
- One of the group had overall accountability for ensuring completion.
- People affected were not kept fully informed.
- Person x was not fully involved.
- The group had different views of what was needed.
- It was not fully debated by the group.
- Members were confused as to what each should do.

Note that all the above points could appear against either reasons for success or failure. What you are trying to do is get the group to analyse the *common factors* that are present irrespective of the specific achievement they are looking at.

It is likely that the syndicates will be very lively, with differences in perspective on which aspects of an initiative were handled well and not so well. Be prepared to allow them to run on if the group is benefiting from the discussion. In this way, members will each be sharing indirectly his or her definition of success, and will be beginning to understand what matters to each person (e.g. things completed on time, everyone pulling their weight, doing what they say they will do etc.).

Part III

Have each syndicate present its conclusions regarding common factors that contribute to success, and common factors that contribute to failure. Allow each syndicate to question and challenge the other to ensure clarity and understanding. Lead a discussion with the group to help them refine the common themes from each presentation, exploring the barriers to their success and what they need to change or do differently. This may result in specific action steps being agreed.

By way of summary, develop a final checklist of Dos and Don'ts for the group that could serve as a guide to help them maximize success and minimize failure in the future. Such a list will be unique to each group and will reflect their special strengths and weaknesses as a team.

Notes

- If the group struggled at times to agree which results were successful and which were not, it may be helpful for them to discuss the general criteria by which they measure success in terms of results and in terms of how they work together. In terms of results, examples of these criteria could include: completion on time; completion to cost; gained commitment of those affected; it works; and seen as successful by others outside the group. In terms of team work, examples could be: members doing what they commit to do; cabinet responsibility once agreed; seen to be supportive by others; commitment versus compliance; and *all* succeed.
- With a small group of 3–5 people, you can choose to do some paired working in Part II or keep the group together and run Parts II and III as an open discussion.
- Because this exercise is focusing on real life issues about which members may have strong views, it is likely that the timescales will be tight. If the group is gaining real value from the discussion, you may wish to adjust the times allowed for Parts II and III.
- Some of the reasons raised for failure may be due to individual members in the group. Whether this will be voiced or not will depend on the levels of openness in the group. It is advisable not to force this and to be sensitive to people being singled out.

Exercise

6

What are the
strengths and
weaknesses? Where
are the opportunities
and threats?

SWOT analysis

Purpose

- To develop a common view of (a) the pressures and challenges associated with the group's tasks and (b) how well equipped they feel they are to meet them.
- To identify actions that will help the group ensure success.

Application

- This is a good general exercise for use at an early stage with a group or with a new project team.
- The outputs will tend to be broad and general but will help the group to concentrate on what its future challenges are and the potential barriers to be overcome.
- For a group, it would be a good precursor to developing specific objectives.

Time required

Total time		1 hour 20 minutes
Part I	Syndicates	20 minutes
Part II	Presentation and discussion	1 hour

Materials needed

- Flipcharts and pens.

Process

Part I

Brief the group on the aims of the exercise and split them into two syndicates. Allow 20 minutes. Ask them to consider the challenges facing the group over the next 12 months and to discuss their answers to the questions below. Ask them to prepare a short (10 minutes maximum) presentation for sharing with the other syndicate. The questions are as follows:

To both syndicates:

- 'What are the main challenges facing us over the next 12 months?'

To syndicate 1:

- 'What do you see as the main strengths of the group that will help us to succeed?'
- 'What are our potential weaknesses that may hinder success?'

To syndicate 2:

- 'What are the main opportunities we could use over the next 6-12 months?'
- 'What are the possible threats or areas of vulnerability?'

The types of answers generated could include the following:

Strengths	Weaknesses
– Committed team.	– React versus plan.
– Hard working.	– All new.
– Technically strong.	– Limited resources.
– Know each other well.	– May take on too much.
– Energetic.	– Much to learn – limited time etc.

Opportunities	Threats
– New products.	– High workload.
– New facilities.	– Inflexible staff.
– Removal of old product lines.	– Legislation.
– Planned programme change.	– Unproven technology.

The nature of the replies, especially if used with a fairly new group, will be very general and broad statements.

Part II

Have each syndicate present back their thoughts, starting with the

'Opportunities and Threats' syndicate first. After each present-ation, ask the rest of the group for any questions or comments, adding to the first syndicate's list if necessary.

Lead a 40-minute discussion with the whole group, using the data shared on the flipcharts, and have them identify some of the actions they may have to take to achieve the following:

- Build on their strengths.
- Reduce the impact of the weaknesses.
- Capitalize on the opportunities.
- Avoid or deal with the threats.

At this stage, keep the discussion fairly general. The aim is to start the group talking and sharing perceptions and identifying common areas of thinking.

Summarize the main conclusions arrived at by the group arrived at on a flipchart. This could be done interactively at the end of the discussion, with the group calling out the conclusions whilst you write them up. Alternatively, you can summarize yourself, based on what you heard, and having taken notes during the discussion.

Variation

- Having taken the initial presentations, you could ask the group to identify from all the data the main barriers to be dealt with. Limit this to three or four barriers. Break the group back into syndicates, allocate the barriers and ask them to work for 45 minutes on possible solutions. Then ask the syndicates to present their solutions to the main group for discussion and agreement. From this point, help the group to develop specific action plans.

Team questionnaires

Purpose

- To allow the group to compare its performance against key criteria for team effectiveness.
- To share individual perceptions and discuss differences in perspective.
- To agree actions to improve performance.

Application

- The method of using a questionnaire against which members rate the team's performance and share scores is perhaps the most commonly used mechanism for reviewing team performance.
- A range of questionnaires (Documents 7.1–7.7) have been included which are increasingly focused on individual behaviours. The more general questionnaires (Documents 7.1–7.3) can be used at any stage. Documents 7.4–7.7 concentrate more on giving individual feedback and will be more useful once the group has started to talk more freely together and develop trust.
- If a questionnaire is used too soon with a group, the tendency is for mid-range scores to be given and true views withheld.
- Choice of which questionnaire to use and when is a matter of judgement dependent on two factors: the stage of development of the group, in particular their current levels of openness and preparedness to give honest feedback; and the nature of the issues within the group.
- Regarding the issues, a questionnaire can be used to 'lead' the group into an area of discussion they might otherwise avoid. For example, if the group's skills are particularly poor with respect to handling conflict, listening etc, the use of Questionnaire 3 ('Assessing Interpersonal Processes') may prove beneficial in stimulating discussion.

Time required

129 Total time   Highly variable: 30 minutes–2 hours.

Materials needed

- Flipcharts and pens.
- Documents 7.1–7.7: one copy per team member of each document being used.

Process

Having selected the questionnaire you wish to use, explain the purpose of the exercise. Hand out the questionnaires and ask members to consider how they see the group operating. Using the questionnaire, ask them to score their current perception, using the factors listed in the questionnaire.

Explain that the questionnaire is subjective, representing their personal view at this point in time. Ask them to be honest in their replies and think of examples that would back up their assessment. Give them 10–15 minutes to complete the questionnaire (dependent on how lengthy and complex it is).

Whilst they are doing this, prepare a summary of the questionnaire on a flipchart. For example, down the left hand side, write single words that summarize the factors listed in the questionnaire (e.g. goals, listening, supporting, participating etc.). When all members have completed their scoring, ask each one to call out his or her scores and write them next to each factor on the flipchart. Do this quickly with no discussion.

When this stage is complete, allow the group to sit back and look at the scores. Ask them to think about any conclusions they can draw. For example, 50 per cent may have scored low on 'commitment to decisions', which begs the question 'Why?'. Ask them to look for wide variations in scores between individuals. It may be useful to circle particularly high or low scores.

Lead the group into a discussion amongst themselves, explaining what the scores are telling them. Encourage individuals to give specific examples from the recent past to explain their scores. Allow the discussion to carry on as long as you feel it is productive. Make them concentrate on the main problem areas they have identified and then ask them to develop actions to address these problems. Once the main issues have been discussed, however, it may be helpful to pause for a moment and summarize those issues on a flipchart before asking the group to develop actions.

What is important is to establish a free discussion, using the outcome of the questionnaire only as the motivation for the process, rather than an end in itself.

Notes

- How long this exercise takes will vary enormously and may not be entirely predictable. Chosen correctly and timed in their use, questionnaires can provide a powerful way of encouraging groups to talk and share hidden perceptions that have been long held.
- With an existing team, the questionnaire could be used at, say, 6-monthly intervals. If scores are kept from previous occasions this will allow the group to assess slippage and progress in the various areas.
- Some of the questionnaires are very simple whilst others have quite specific behavioural ranges described. The former are useful with a low-risk or 'closed' group or with a very open group who only need a simple prompt. The more specific questionnaires should be introduced at the 'storming' stage to prevent avoidance, opting out or sweeping statements that cannot be justified. They help to focus the members' thinking and force specific objective data into the discussion.

Variation

- A simple variation is to ask the group to generate their own rating scale first. This can be done in open discussion by having the group state the main criteria for measuring team effectiveness. List them and simplify the answers to about a dozen factors or less. Then ask the group to rate themselves against those factors.

Document 7.1

Assessing Group Effectiveness

The following are examples of the elements to be assessed in developing team performance.

Consider where your own team's performance scores on the following scales. Please circle an appropriate scale value.

1) Communication ability

Guarded, cautious.   *1 2 3 4 5 6 7*   Open, honest.

2) Feelings of mutual support

Each man for himself, highly individualistic.   *1 2 3 4 5 6 7*   Genuine concern for others, high cohesion.

3) Group goals

Poor, not understood.   *1 2 3 4 5 6 7*   Clear to all, understood and commited to.

4) Handling conflicts

Use of denial, avoidance, suppression.   *1 2 3 4 5 6 7*   Face up to conflicts, differences expressed and tackled.

5) Trust between individuals

Withholding of information, low trust and suspicion.   *1 2 3 4 5 6 7*   Common sharing of information, high trust.

6) Control

Control is imposed, high use of authority.   *1 2 3 4 5 6 7*   Self-control, high levels of self-direction and shared decision making.

7) Use of resources

Poor usage, duplication and time wasting.   *1 2 3 4 5 6 7*   Fully used, work interdependently.

8) Leadership

Group leadership needs not met.   *1 2 3 4 5 6 7*   Needs met – leadership accepted and respected.

9) Participation and commitment

Few dominate, cliquish, low commitment to team.   *1 2 3 4 5 6 7*   High participation and commitment to team.

Reproduced from *Building a Better Team*, by Peter Moxon, Gower, Aldershot, 1993.

Document 7.2

Team Effectiveness Rating Questionnaire

Under each of the following factors below please ring the number which most closely corresponds to your assessment of the team's current operation.

Ineffective   **Effective**

Objectives

1 2 3 4 5 6 7 8 9

Vague; confused; contradictory; inappropriate; little interest; not worked to or valued.

Clear to all; viable; understood and committed to by all; regularly reviewed.

Problem solving

1 2 3 4 5 6 7 8 9

Jump to conclusions; remedial action; deal with effects rather than causes; failure to define the problem.

Clear diagnosis of situation and effects; identification of causes; consider alternative solutions before action agreed.

Creativity/innovation

1 2 3 4 5 6 7 8 9

Little attempt to look at problem in new ways; only used tried and tested methods; resistance to new ideas – home in on negatives; defensive and reluctant to change.

Creativity encouraged; new ideas continually sought; focus on improvement; individuals flexible and receptive to suggestions; support and build on each other's contributions.

Approach to task

1 2 3 4 5 6 7 8 9

Reactive; undisciplined; digression and loss of direction; action- versus results-oriented; fragmented discussion; domination by minority; poor listening.

Systematic and self-disciplined; think before acting; logical and considered approach; co-ordinated discussions; all team members involved; attentive listening.

Decision making

1 2 3 4 5 6 7 8 9

Necessary decisions not made or delayed; decisions made by a minority – others not involved or committed; quick to decide without proper evaluation.

Appropriate people involved; easy consensus on most issues; diversity and difference of view used to improve quality of decisions; decisions 'considered' but never ducked.

Reproduced from *Building a Better Team*, by Peter Moxon, Gower, Aldershot, 1993.

Leadership

1 2 3 4 5 6 7 8 9

Group and individual needs for leadership not met; abdication of leadership or dominant leader controlling all key decisions; compliance is the norm; leader does not tolerate challenge to authority.

Leadership shared by group; different individuals assume the role when appropriate – not always the appointed leader; participation and co-operation actively encouraged.

Feelings

1 2 3 4 5 6 7 8 9

Feelings ignored; individuals not encouraged to share feelings; no risk taking; personal views dismissed, attacked or not thought a relevant part of teamworking.

Feelings freely expressed without fear; displayed empathy and understanding prevalent; individuals sensitive to others' needs or concerns; openness encouraged.

Group cohesion

1 2 3 4 5 6 7 8 9

Restrictive pressure towards conformity and compliance; team members act as individuals pursuing own goals; minimum support given to each other.

Relaxed, open atmosphere; high levels of mutual respect and support; co-operative working and collaboration; group identity seen as important.

Trust

1 2 3 4 5 6 7 8 9

Team members suspicious / wary of each other; true thoughts often withheld; individuals guarded in what they say; overtly will agree and comply whilst inwardly rejecting decisions and ideas; critical of each other but opinions expressed only in private.

Individuals trust each other; benefit of doubt always given; individuals share private thoughts without fear of reprisal or abuse of confidence; high level of candour and feedback.

Accountability/commitment

1 2 3 4 5 6 7 8 9

Individuals avoid acceptance of responsibility; individuals quick to apportion blame and pass on responsibility; low reliability of follow-through; more talk than action.

Individuals and the group commit themselves to action; high reliability of follow-through; strong sense of 'cabinet' responsibility; take on whatever is necessary to achieve the task.

List other comments on a separate sheet if necessary.

Reproduced from *Building a Better Team*, by Peter Moxon, Gower, Aldershot, 1993.

| **Document 7.3** | **Assessing Interpersonal Processes Questionnaire** |

To what extent do team members . . .

1) Listen effectively to each other (by summarizing and not interrupting)?

1	2	3	4	5
Not at all	To a small extent	Moderate extent	Great extent	Very great extent

2) Support one another (by assuming others' ideas have merit, providing positive feedback and building on their ideas)?

1	2	3	4	5
Not at all	To a small extent	Moderate extent	Great extent	Very great extent

3) Differ constructively with one another (by stating differences of opinion without implying the other is wrong)?

1	2	3	4	5
Not at all	To a small extent	Moderate extent	Great extent	Very great extent

4) Participate equally in the discussion (by openly expressing their own ideas and opinions)?

1	2	3	4	5
Not at all	To a small extent	Moderate extent	Great extent	Very great extent

5) Discuss how well the group is functioning (by periodically reviewing the process and behaviours of individuals)?

1	2	3	4	5
Not at all	To a small extent	Moderate extent	Great extent	Very great extent

Reproduced from *Building a Better Team*, by Peter Moxon, Gower, Aldershot, 1993.

Team Climate Questionnaire

Under each of the following factors below please ring the number which most realistically represents your assessment of the team's current climate.

1) Openness

Are individuals open in their transactions with each other? Are there hidden agendas? Can team members express their feelings about others openly without offence?

| People are very guarded about expressing their views or feelings. | *1 2 3 4 5 6 7 8 9* | Individuals are very open in expressing their views and feelings. |

2) Conformity

How rigid is the group in adhering to the procedures and methods it has adopted? Is the group flexible in its thinking? Does it require strict rules to work to?

| The group conforms strictly to a set pattern of working. | *1 2 3 4 5 6 7 8 9* | The group is flexible and adapts itself effectively to changing situations. |

3) Confronting/hiding

Are difficult and uncomfortable issues worked through? Are conflicts swept under the carpet or confronted? How much energy does the group give to resolving disagreements and difficulties openly?

| Many difficulties and uncomfortable issues get avoided. | *1 2 3 4 5 6 7 8 9* | The group deals with problems openly as they arise. |

4) Supportiveness

Are group members sensitive to each other's needs? What happens when an individual makes a msitake? How much energy do group members give to help each other?

| Individuals can expect little help from others. | *1 2 3 4 5 6 7 8 9* | There is high group support for individuals. |

Reproduced from *Building a Better Team*, by Peter Moxon, Gower, Aldershot, 1993.

5) Risk taking

Are individuals encouraged to try out new things and risk possible failure or ridicule? Does the team positively encourage people to extend themselves?

The team does not encourage   *1 2 3 4 5 6 7 8 9*   Experimentation, new
risk taking.   ventures and personal
                                                   exploration are the norm.

6) Energy

How high is the energy level of the group? To what extent is the energy of team members directed towards improving team performance?

Team members cannot be   *1 2 3 4 5 6 7 8 9*   There is a high level of energy
bothered directing much   for improving team
energy into making the team   performance.
better.

7) Personal and team development

Are the standards that the group sets itself for behaviours high? Are dysfunctional behaviours and poor team operation tolerated? Does the group take responsibility for its own development and learning?

The group sets itself low   *1 2 3 4 5 6 7 8 9*   The standards set are high
standards and individuals   and every opportunity to
take no responsibility for   learn and progress is taken.
their own learning.

Other comments

_____

_____

_____

_____

_____

_____

_____

_____

_____

_____

Influencing Team Meetings Questionnaire

Examine the following behaviours and circle the number which you feel describes how much of that behaviour you display.

Using a second sheet have each other team member circle how *they* see your behaviours.

	Little or none	Some		A lot
1. Puts forward ideas and proposals for action.	1	2	3	4	5
2. Brings in others and facilitates introduction of facts and information.	1	2	3	4	5
3. Shows interest, enthusiasm and high participation.	1	2	3	4	5
4. Supports and encourages others.	1	2	3	4	5
5. Reduces tension when it arises.	1	2	3	4	5
6. Mediates differences by offering compromises and seeking alternatives.	1	2	3	4	5
7. Recognizes, elaborates and builds on others' contributions.	1	2	3	4	5
8. Keeps the group focused on the task and use of time.	1	2	3	4	5
9. Listens and clarifies issues.	1	2	3	4	5
10. Summarizes discussions, focusing the flow of the discussion.	1	2	3	4	5
11. Challenges assumptions and generalizations.	1	2	3	4	5
12. Confronts others and helps .manage conflicts.	1	2	3	4	5

Team Leadership Questionnaire

In your view how do you see the team leader's behaviour with the team? Using the descriptions below, score a rating on each scale.

Distrust of subordinates; minimal confidence in his/her abilities.	*1 2 3 4 5 6 7*	Displays a high level of trust and confidence in the team's abilities.
Exerts a high level of control; takes or sanctions all key decisions; minimal delegation.	*1 2 3 4 5 6 7*	High level of delegation of actions and decision making; exerts minimal control; provides help and support where needed.
Intolerant of challenges to authority; suppresses argument or dissent.	*1 2 3 4 5 6 7*	Encourages challenge; sees difference in view as healthy; encourages openness.
Deals with team on a one-to-one basis; minimal joint team working.	*1 2 3 4 5 6 7*	Deals with team as a cohesive unit; encourages collaboration and joint working.
Unaware of own impact on the team; seeks no feedback; discourages comment.	*1 2 3 4 5 6 7*	Self-aware; actively seeks feedback on own impact; receptive to others' ideas and comments.
Remains distant from the team; communication on business issues only; reveals little of self or personal views and feelings.	*1 2 3 4 5 6 7*	Develops close relationship with team; informal relaxed approach; encourages openness and shares own concerns on occasions.
Highly task-focused; uncompromising and demanding; intolerant of failure.	*1 2 3 4 5 6 7*	Creates climate for creativity and innovation; encourages risk taking; tolerates 'failure' and uses it to learn from.
Sees training as secondary; spends no time developing members' potential.	*1 2 3 4 5 6 7*	Actively develops individuals; spends time coaching and helping individuals grow.

Minimal concern for subordinates; indifferent to their needs and concerns.	*1 2 3 4 5 6 7*	High concern for individuals; active interest in their concerns and worries and helping individuals handle them.
Sets firm targets for individuals; expects delivery; intolerant of failure; provides minimal support.	*1 2 3 4 5 6 7*	Jointly agrees objectives with individual and team; gains commitment; works with team to ensure achievement; coaching and helping where necessary.
Inwardly focused; parochial with regard to own 'patch'; minimal interest in other areas; formal relationships with other areas.	*1 2 3 4 5 6 7*	Outwardly focused; views own area as a part of the 'whole'; builds strong working relationships with other areas.

Overall contribution to team effectiveness

1 2 3 4 5 6 7

Reproduced from *Building a Better Team*, by Peter Moxon, Gower, Aldershot, 1993.

Behaviour Feedback Questionnaire

Read through the statements below and select the two team members whose current behaviours best fit the descriptions when compared to the whole group. Write their names in the spaces provided. Make sure you write down two names but do not include yourself (though you may wish privately to consider which descriptions best fit your own behaviours).

Which two members of the group:

1) can most easily influence the rest of the group?   _____   _____

2) support and protect other members who are under attack?   _____   _____

3) are most highly accepted within the group?   _____   _____

4) clash most sharply during meetings?   _____   _____

5) contribute most to discussions?   _____   _____

6) contribute least to discussions?   _____   _____

7) can be relied upon most to meet commitments?   _____   _____

8) are least reliable?   _____   _____

9) are least able to influence the group?   _____   _____

10) are more likely to put their own objectives before the group's objectives?   _____   _____

11) are more likely to put the group's objectives before their own?   _____   _____

Reproduced from *Building a Better Team*, by Peter Moxon, Gower, Aldershot, 1993.

12) have the greatest desire to achieve? _____ _____

13) have the most balanced judgement? _____ _____

14) most want to avoid conflict situations? _____ _____

15) withdraw most when conflict arises? _____ _____

16) compete the most? _____ _____

17) try to keep the discussions on track? _____ _____

18) do you find it easiest to work with? _____ _____

19) do you find it hardest to work with? _____ _____

20) do you understand least? _____ _____

Reproduced from *Building a Better Team*,
by Peter Moxon, Gower, Aldershot, 1993.

What do individuals
do that helps or
hinders team
performance?

Helping and hindering

Purpose

- To provide constructive feedback to members on how they
  affect the team.
- To develop individual action plans to address issues.

Application

- This exercise is best introduced once the group has progressed
  through the 'storming' stage and has started to develop an
  attitude of collaboration and openness.
- Used too soon, the responses will be bland and unhelpful,
  with members withholding real views or, at the other extreme,
  being destructive and unhelpful.
- This is a potentially threatening exercise for some people. To
  gain maximum benefit *all* team members must be relatively
  comfortable receiving personal feedback and must be capable
  of giving helpful feedback to others.

Time required

Total time		2–3 hours
Part I	Individual working	30 minutes
Part II	Sharing perspectives	1 hour 30 minutes
Part III	Action planning	1 hour

Materials needed

- Writing paper and pens.

Process

Part I

Explain that the purpose of the exercise is to provide an opportunity

to understand better the impact each member has on the team's performance and to develop individual actions to improve each contribution to the team. Emphasize that the aim is for each member to help the others through honest and open feedback.

Explain that initially you want each individual to think about how they view the behaviours of each other member of the group. In particular:

- In what ways do they help the group working?
- In what ways do they hinder the group working?

Ask the group members to note down their answers to these questions for each other member *and* for themselves. Tell them to be specific and describe what they see the other person *doing*. The more descriptive the feedback, the more helpful it will be. Give them some examples: 'One of the things I find unhelpful is that you always turn up late for meetings'. This is *factual and specific*, as opposed to: 'You are not committed to team meetings' which is *a conclusion* that could be argued over. (Depending on the group, you may want at this stage to provide a short input on giving and receiving feedback – see 'Notes for the facilitator' below.) Ask them to be honest and to focus on the things which are most important to the effectiveness of their working relationships (see Part I, Chapter 1, 'How are trust and openness developed?').

Split the group up for individual working and allow them 30 minutes (or more with a large group) to think through their answers. Explain that when they reconvene you will be asking them to share their deliberations.

The group may be very nervous at this stage and go quiet. Some individuals will crack a joke to try to reduce the tension. It is a hard exercise, even for a mature group; most individuals are good at experiencing feelings (e.g. 'He annoys me – I get angry') but find it difficult when asked to specify what behaviour is causing the anger. Not many people are good observers of behaviour, but an important part of the team process is to help them develop this skill and, moreover, give skilful feedback.

When the group reconvenes, take one person in turn and have them share, informally, their feedback with the rest of the group. Allow only questions of clarification from others at this stage. Encourage members to make their own notes as opposed to charting any of the data. Help each one by probing and asking for examples if his or her statements are vague or fairly meaningless – but be sensitive.

Once all the data has been shared, each person will have several perspectives of his or her behaviour. Explain that you now want the group to have an open discussion where members can query what has been said about them in order to gain further understanding. (In your planning allow up to 10 minutes per person.) Try to encourage a free flowing discussion and help members to make the most of the opportunity. Ask them how they feel about what has been said.

The facilitator's role is the key to a quality debate in these circumstances. On the one hand, you must have as low a profile as possible, but, on the other hand, you must intervene to keep the discussion on track and of high quality. It is easy for members to deflect and rationalize the feedback in order to avoid accepting it. Allow the discussion to run as long as the group is finding it productive. Make sure all members have a chance to review their feedback.

Part II

Once the discussion comes naturally to an end, introduce the last part of the exercise. Explain that you want each member to develop a simple action plan to address issues raised in their feedback.

Ask them to work in pairs, reflect on their feedback and list one or two examples of how they plan to act differently in the future. Ask them to be specific and realistic with each action listed, as follows:

- What are they going to do?
- How will they measure their success?
- What method will they use?
- What help do they need from the group?

Allow approximately 40 minutes for this part and have them test their plan with their partner. At the end, have each person quickly share his or her plan with the whole group. It would be beneficial to the group if copies of the plans were collated and redistributed to all group members after the team session, for review in the future.

A sample action plan is outlined as follows:

– Action	To be more succinct at presentations.
– Measuring success	Ask for feedback from the group after my next presentation.
– What method	Prepare more thoroughly rather than improvising; use less material; and attend a presentation skills workshop in the next 6 months.
– What help	Immediate, honest feedback – and suggestions! And review progress with the group after next presentation.

Variations

An alternative set of questions to ask during Part I is as follows:

- What do you want the other person to do more of?
- What do you want the other person to do less of?
- What do you want the other person to do differently?

Notes for the facilitator on constructive feedback

Feedback is a way of learning more about ourselves and the effect our behaviour has on others. Constructive feedback increases self-awareness, offers options and encourages development, so it can be important to learn to give it and receive it. Constructive feedback does not mean only positive feedback; negative feedback, given skilfully, can be very important and helpful. On the other hand, destructive feedback is feedback that is given in an unskilled way which leaves the recipient simply feeling bad with seemingly nothing on which to build or options for using the data.

Giving skilled feedback

1. Start with the positive   Everyone needs encouragement – to be told when they are doing something right. If the positive is registered first, any negative feedback is more likely to be listened to and acted upon. For example: 'I liked the way you were prepared to consider Bill's view. However, every time Jane and Michael made a suggestion you immediately disagreed and did not seem willing to listen to them.' Our culture tends to emphasize the negative and we are too quick to blame when something goes wrong. In the rush to criticize, it is all too easy to overlook the good things. Concentrating first on the positive has an additional benefit as individual weaknesses often stem from exaggerated strengths. For example, if a person is overly enthusiastic they can be poor listeners or if they are too task-focused they may appear impatient and insensitive to others. Thus talking first about strengths provides a natural lead to discussing how those strengths, in some situations, become real weaknesses.

2. Be descriptive rather than evaluative   When giving feedback tell the person what you saw or what they did and describe what effect it had, rather than state that something was good or bad. For example, 'You sounded hesitant in your reply and I was left thinking you were not in total agreement with what was said.' If you describe observable behaviours, arguments are less likely to develop.

However, evaluative phrases – for example, 'you are lazy' or 'you are not commited' – report conclusions or interpretations and are open to easy disagreement by the recipient of the feedback.

3. Own the feedback   It is important to take responsibility for any feedback given. Begin with phrases such as 'I find that . . .' or 'One of the difficulties I experience is when you . . .'. Avoid phrases such as 'Others think that . . .' or 'It is said that . . .' as ways of distancing yourself from the statement. Such generalized comments are again easily challengeable and somewhat unhelpful.

4. Offer alternatives   When negative feedback is offered make sure suggestions are also offered as to what the individual should do differently. 'When you are late for meetings it wastes everybody's time waiting for you. It would be helpful if, when you are delayed elsewhere, you phoned through a message so we can decide whether to start without you or not.'

5. Always leave the recipient with a choice   The aim of feedback is to help increase the self-awareness of the recipient and to provide an opportunity for learning. The choice of whether to accept such comments, however, must rest with the person concerned. Imposing feedback will invite resistance or rejection. All we can ask is that the person listens and understands the feedback and takes time to reflect on it. We have no right to insist that he or she changes simply to suit our needs. It may also help to examine the consequences for the person if he or she does not, but that does not mean prescribing change or threatening sanctions for non-conformance!

6. Think what the feedback you give says about you   Feedback is likely to say as much about the giver as the receiver. For example, an organized person is more likely to be frustrated by others who are disorganized. When we give feedback it says much about our own values and what we consider significant in others. Therefore, when giving feedback make sure that you differentiate between what you want the other person to do that will help, and proposals that are simply meant to make that person like yourself. Also concentrate only on the changes that are important rather than cosmetic.

Receiving feedback

If we are on the receiving end of feedback from others there are some precautions we can take that will encourage the giver to use the skills outlined above.

1. Listen to what is said without rejecting or arguing with it   Feedback can be uncomfortable but we are the poorer without it. To listen to and understand what is said does not always mean we must agree with it. It does, however, require us to think about it, and that requires conscious effort and concentration. This is especially so when the comments are personal and likely to evoke strong feelings within us. Try to avoid jumping to conclusions or becoming immediately defensive. If you do, others will stop giving the feedback and the opportunites to learn about yourself will be reduced.

2. Be clear about what is actually being said   Make sure you understand what is being said before you respond. Hear the other person out fully and then ask questions to test understanding. For example, 'So what you are saying is . . . ?'

3. Check the feedback with others   Do not rely on one source alone. Ask if others have the same perspective or problems. Others may experience us differently or may see the same behaviour in us but it affects them differently. This helps us to keep individual comments in context and to understand the scale of any problems we may be causing.

4. Actively seek and encourage feedback   Each of us needs to know how other people experience us. People may think things without telling us, particularly if we do not make it easy for them to do so. We must therefore actively seek the views of others on how they perceive our behaviours. If we do so regularly, it will encourage and make it easier for others to raise any issues that may develop in the future.

5. Decide what you will do as a result of the feedback   The choice of whether to accept or reject feedback always rests with the receiver. However, continuously ignoring what is said, and not acting on any aspect of it, is the quickest way of ensuring that feedback will cease. As individuals we will not change our personality easily. What we can do is modify and control our behaviours to the benefit of ourselves and others. In reality, to significantly improve our interaction with others will only require us to change our actions in some 10–20 per cent of the situations we get into. For the remainder of the time there is unlikely to be a problem. In addition, others will respond positively and with a far higher degree of tolerance and support if we are seen to try, even though our efforts may at times fail or appear somewhat forced.

Finally, be sure to thank the person for his or her comments; we might benefit from them. Feedback may not be easy to give but it is a valuable practice to be reinforced and encouraged within any team, for it forms part of the bedrock of team effectiveness.

Individual challenges and pressures

Purpose

- To develop a better appreciation across the group of how each person sees their role and the challenges and pressures facing them.

Application

- This is a good exercise for both existing or relatively new teams.
- It is a non-threatening exercise and can be used at the start of the teambuilding programme to encourage levels of openness. It is likely to be used as a once-off exercise.
- At first sight the exercise may seem to be unnecessary with long-standing teams, but even at that stage it is surprising how little appreciation members have of each other's situations.
- It provides a good opportunity for members to gain real appreciation within the group of the pressures and problems they are facing and the help and tolerance they each may need from other members.

Time required

Total time   20 minutes per team member (e.g. 3 hours for a group of 8).

Members will also need to complete 30–40 minutes' pre-work before the session.

Materials needed

- Pre-work Briefing Sheet (Document 9.1).
- Presentation materials (flipchart, pens, acetate).

Process

The exercise involves each team member giving a 15-minute formal presentation to the group. If it is included within a half- or one-day team session, individuals will need to prepare their presentations before the session; use the Briefing Sheet (Document 9.1). In a 2–3 day team session, you may instead wish to plan in 30 minutes to 1 hour during the session for individuals to prepare their presentations. Which method you choose will depend on the objectives of the session and the best use of the time. In either case, it is important to brief the team on the expected content.

Ask them to prepare, for formal presentation, a 15-minute talk addressing the following questions about their current role:

- What are the main challenges facing them over the next 12 months?
- What are the main barriers and difficulties that they will have to tackle?
- What particular help do they need from the team?

Stress that you are not looking for a simple list of their current objectives and an outline job description.

The aim of the session is to allow members to give the group a real appreciation of what challenges and pressures they are facing over the next year. It is an opportunity for each member to indicate to the rest of the group the size of the task facing him or her and how he or she feels about it. Is it going to be easy, or very difficult? Does he or she require general tolerance from the group or direct help from specific members in order to achieve his or her objectives?

What is important is that the group as a whole is left with a good appreciation of how each member *feels*. It is those feelings that will affect the member's future behaviour within the group. Knowing how he or she feels will help the group better understand and tolerate the resulting behaviours (e.g. poor time-keeping resulting from pressure, frustration or preoccupation with matters outside a meeting).

When all members have prepared their presentations, introduce the aim of the exercise and allow *15 minutes for each presentation and 5 minutes for any questions by the group*. You will need to be firm with the time schedule and keep questions to those of clarification. Do not allow the session to degenerate into discussion of any business issues that may be brought up. It is very likely that most will struggle with the 15-minute limit and bring too much material to share. We all like to talk about our job, pressures and problems! With a large group, especially, keeping to the schedule is crucial if the session is not to become laborious. Group the talks in threes and plan breaks after each hour. A group of 8 will take 3 hours to complete their presentations. (With a group of over 8, it may be better to plan a second session or reduce the inputs to 10 minutes only and target four presentations per hour.)

If you plan the exercise within a 2–3 day session, members can pursue their conversations during the evening, which can be extremely productive.

Variation

– With a new team (e.g. a project team), a variation on the questions above that focuses on the content of their role may be more useful as follows:

What do they see as the primary purpose of their job?
What are their areas of responsibility?
What are the main relationships with others that are important to them doing their job?

– If appropriate the exercise can be extended by one and a half hours to allow the group to break up into smaller groups or pairs to continue discussion. Ask each member to write down which three people he or she would like to spend more time with, and then collect the answers. Allow the group a 15-minute break whilst you work out suitable sub-groups. When they return, announce the sub-groupings and then allow them an hour to discuss whatever they wish within their own sub-groups.

Document 9.1

Briefing Sheet

As part of the next session, please prepare a presentation addressing the following questions about your current role:

- What are the main challenges facing you over the next 12 months?
- What are the main barriers and difficulties that you will have to tackle?
- What particular help do you need from the team?

Your presentation should not take more than 15 minutes and there will be a further 5 minutes for you to answer any questions.

The aim of the exercise is to provide you with an opportunity to give your colleagues a *real* appreciation of the challenges and pressures of your job as you see them and how you feel about the situation (e.g. Is the next year going to be difficult or easy? Are you confident or unsure about success? Do you just require tolerance of your situation from the group or will you need specific help from individual members?).

Please keep the presentation to 15 minutes.

Focus on the important issues and events that matter to you and that you believe will be helpful to the group.

Reproduced from *Building a Better Team*, by Peter Moxon, Gower, Aldershot, 1993.

**Exercise
10**

What do team
members expect of
each other?

Expectations exchange

Purpose

- To clarify expectations between different teams or between sub-groups within a single team.
- To agree actions to address problem areas.

Application

- The exercise is particularly useful for sharing perceptions between two groups and helping them to clarify how they need to work together to be effective. It provides a structured way for the groups (a) to share feedback on how they view both themselves and the other group and (b) to work together to address any issues.
- Participants can be two separate teams who interact closely (e.g. separate engineering and production teams), or two sub-groups within a single team.
- The exercise can be used at any stage of a group's development but is especially helpful at the 'forming' and 'storming' stages.
- Used at the 'forming' stage, it can help prevent misinterpretation and misunderstanding. Used at the 'storming' stage, it can help solve these problems.

Time required

Total time		Up to 4 hours
Part I	Syndicate working	1 hour
	Presentation and discussion	1 hour 30 minutes
Part II	Syndicate working	45 minutes
	Presentation and discussion	45 minutes

Materials needed

- Flipchart, pad and pens.
- Syndicate Briefing Sheet (Document 10.1).

Process

Brief the group on the aims of the exercise and explain that there are two parts to the exercise. The first part will involve them initially working in their *own* syndicates made up of their own functional groups (e.g. engineering and production teams) as they share perceptions of each other. The second part will involve working in mixed syndicates as they agree action plans to address issues raised in Part I.

Part I

Allocate rooms to each syndicate, give out the Briefing Sheet (Document 10.1) and ask each syndicate to prepare their answers to the following two sets of questions:

- What do they expect to get from the other group?
- What do they not expect to get from the other group?
- How do they see the current situation with regard to the above?

- What do they expect to give the other group?
- What do they not expect to give the other group?
- How do they see the current situation with regard to the above?

Ask them to prepare a 15-minute presentation, summarizing the conclusions of their discussion, to share with the other group. Allow up to 1 hour for the syndicate work.

Reconvene the whole group and allow each syndicate 20 minutes to give their presentations and answer questions of clarification. Do not allow them to start debating the issues until both syndicates have given their presentations. Also, do not allow either syndicate to start defending or rationalizing their behaviours. The aim at this point is to get them to listen and reflect on the feedback given.

Once both presentations are complete lead an open discussion with the group, and have them review the presentations in more depth. Help the group identify the main issues that need to be worked on and list these on a flipchart. Make the group prioritize the list and choose the top four issues that, if resolved, would most increase effectiveness.

Part II

Split the group into two mixed syndicates composed of equal

members of each functional group. Give each syndicate two of the issues to work on. Brief them to explore the issues further, identifying the causes and recommending action plans. Ask them to detail what actions are needed, who is responsible, and what timescales are involved, and to agree how the problem can be prevented from recurring. Allow the syndicates 45 minutes to 1 hour to work on the issues and prepare a short presentation of their recommendations.

Reconvene the whole group and have each syndicate present their recommendations for discussion and agreement. Make sure a written record, for typing and distribution, is made of the final action plans agreed.

Finally, have the whole group agree on how they will monitor and review progress against their actions. This agreement is vital if you are dealing with two separate teams in the group.

Notes

- If the exercise is being run with two separate teams, it is worth briefing them to prepare their initial presentation before they arrive. This will allow maximum time for discussion and agreement.
- This exercise can be run as a full teambuilding session on its own. If this is the case, or if you are dealing with two separate teams, it is advisable to start the whole session off with an exercise on expectations and ground rules to settle the group down and help ensure that constructive feedback is given during the day (see Exercise 2). It would also be valuable in this case to allow 15 minutes at the end of the day for a quick review with the group on how they felt about the session.

Variation

- An alternative simpler set of questions can be used for Part I as follows:

    What is their image of the other group and why?
    What image do they think the other group has of their group and why?
    What problems, if addressed, would improve the relationship between the two groups?

Document 10.1

Briefing Sheet

The aim of this exercise is to allow you to consider how you view the effectiveness of your syndicate's working relationship with the other syndicate, and in what ways it could be improved.

As a group, discuss your answers to the two sets of questions below, which will help you define what it is you expect of the other syndicate and how you see the current situation.

Prepare a 15-minute presentation, summarizing the conclusions of your discussion, to share with the other group. Please include a few specific examples to support your conclusions.

Set 1

    – What do you expect to get from the other group?
    – What do you not expect to get from the other group?
    – How do you see the current situation with regard to the above?

Set 2

    – What do you expect to give the other group?
    – What do you not expect to give the other group?
    – How do you see the current situation with regard to the above?

Please be honest and constructive in your presentation and try to identify some of the key issues that need to be worked on.

You have .... to complete your discussions and prepare your presentation.

Reproduced from *Building a Better Team*, by Peter Moxon, Gower, Aldershot, 1993.

Exercise
11

How does a new
member of the team
settle in quickly?

Introducing a new player

Purpose

- To help a new member to settle into the team quickly and establish his or her role.

Application

- This is more a coaching activity than a group exercise, and it can be carried out by the team leader or a neutral facilitator to help a new member to settle quickly into the team.
- This activity is helpful when a member joins an existing team or takes up a new role within a team. It is also very useful when a member is given a project leader role, in a situation where other members' expectations of him or her may already be fairly fixed.
- It needs to be carried out with the individual concerned during the first 1–2 months, either as a single session or a series of short sessions.
- The Coaching Checklist (Document 11.1) provides a series of questions which, if worked through and answered, will help prevent misplaced expectations within the team and potential problems in the future. This checklist can be issued simply as a prompt sheet for the individual to use on his or her own without coaching, but, used in this way, it is unlikely to be as successful.

Time required

Total time   6–8 hours spread over the first 2 months.

Materials needed

- Coaching Checklist (Document 11.1).

Background

From the first day that a new member joins a team, expectations will start to build up, both in the team and in the individual, regarding the new player's role and how he or she should operate. Indeed, the rest of the team will also have preconceived notions based on how the previous incumbent operated. Motivating the new member to think through such issues early on and share them with the team can prevent early misunderstandings caused by any misplaced expectations.

Once a new member has been in place for 3–6 months, a view of his or her way of operating will have formed in the team's mind (e.g. 'He's quiet and keeps to himself; I never see him'; 'He just does what he thinks is right and never consults'). Such behaviours may well be due to the pressures of coming to terms with a new job and not truly reflect how the person wants to be viewed. By then, however, it can be too late. Views have been formed that will be difficult to change.

This situation can be pre-empted, however, by using the Coaching Checklist (Document 11.1) provided and prompting the member to think *actively* about his or her role and positively manage the early relationships with the other team members.

The checklist will influence people to think through important issues that they may otherwise not formally consider (e.g. how to define success for themselves, how to understand others' perceptions of what success looks like, and how to communicate the way he or she intends to operate). Whilst the questions on the checklist may appear obvious, few members bother to review the situation in their first months in the job and search for the answers. Most become immediately inolved in the day-to-day activity, surfacing some months later to wonder why they are not in control or why others are disappointed with their contribution.

Process

With a new project leader

The best way to use the checklist with individual members assigned to lead a project is to plan a day with them in the first week of their assignment.

Work through each of the areas on the Coaching Checklist (Document 11.1) and use it to *make them think*. It is unlikely that they will be able to give answers to all the questions but, at this stage, ascertain their first thoughts. Going through the checklist will cause them to do things in the first few weeks that they may not otherwise have thought about (e.g. trying to define how others will measure their success, and deciding how they are going to make

158

sure, from the start, that others do not have unreasonable or erroneous expectations of them). At the very least, make them consider all the main issues they will deal with, and have them collect data on what their colleagues are expecting and discuss these data with them.

Following the initial session, plan another after 4 weeks to review progress and check they are addressing the factors that emerged in the first meeting.

With new team members or members taking on changed roles

In these circumstances, there are two ways of using the Coaching Checklist (Document 11.1), as follows:

- Give the list to the individual team member during their first 2–3 days in the job, and talk them through it so that they understand the questions. Ask them over the next 4 weeks to think through their answers. Arrange a full day at the end of the month with them when they can be expected to work through the answers with you (or the team leader). You may ask them to prepare their answers to each section as a formal presentation (i.e. the role definition, success criteria, challenges and difficulties). Half-way though the month, check how they are progressing.
- Alternatively arrange a series of weekly 2-hour sessions with the individual, starting from the end of the first month. At each session, work through some of the questions with them and agree any actions. For example:

Week 5	A	Role definition/success criteria
	B	Challenges and difficulties
Week 6	C	Relationships
	D	Launching their role
Week 7	E	Training needs
	F	Action plans

- The action plans developed in the final session will be a summary of the various plans agreed at the end of each session, plus any others you both feel are necessary. If done this way, make sure all the ground is covered within 6–8 weeks.

To help the individual concerned, explain to the team that he or she is going to take the first 2 months to settle into the job and will use the time to clarify and finalize his or her objectives and role. As part of the individual's action plan, make sure that he or she arranges in the third month to share appropriate outcomes from your coaching sessions with the team. This will enable him or her formally to 'launch' his or her role within the team.

Also ensure that the individual spends some time with all other team members during the first 2 months, collecting data on how the team see his or her role – that is, the 'Relationships' section in the checklist. This will greatly help the individual to understand where his or her own expectations differ from those of the team. For example, one team member may be wanting unreasonably fast attention on an issue. Being aware of any mismatches in advance will allow the individual either to change his or her plans or to revise the team's expectations.

Notes

- Your role must be one of questioning the individual and making him or her think, rather than providing the answers. It is often worthwhile using a flipchart as you are working and list the answers. A good session is likely to end up repapering the room! Also the act of writing down the answers will help crystallize the individual's thinking, and will ensure that his or her answers are specific as opposed to vague notions.
- If the team leader conducts the sessions, make sure he or she understands that his or her role is to coach, and not to instruct by providing the answers. Follow up to see that this is happening.

Coaching Checklist

Role definition/success criteria

- How does the individual view his or her role? What does he or she see as its primary purpose and what are the key result areas?
- How does he or she personally want to benefit from the assignment? What will success look like in 6 months' time in terms of results and in terms of how he or she will go about the job?
- How will he or she measure and review his or her success?

Challenges and difficulties

- What does he or she see as the main challenges to be tackled in the first 6 months? Which is the single biggest challenge?
- What are the main barriers and challenges? How does he or she plan to address them?

Relationships

- With whom does he or she need to develop effective relationships? Which areas, which individuals? How will he or she achieve this?
- What are his or her expectations with regard to the team? What will he or she give to the team? What will he or she want from the team?
- What do they see as the team's expectations of them? How will they check this out or uncover such expectations?

Launching their role

- Having answered the previous questions, how will he or she communicate his or her role and the initial priorities:

  To the team?
  To others who need to know?

Reproduced from *Building a Better Team*,
by Peter Moxon, Gower, Aldershot, 1993.

– In what ways does the individual think he or she can best establish his or her role during the first 6 months? What are the impact areas?

Training needs

– What skills will be needed to ensure success? Where will he or she need training or help?
– In particular, what help will he or she most need from the other team members and the team leader?

Action plans

– What is their action plan to:

Communicate their role to others?
Finalize and communicate their objectives for the first 6 months?
Start to build effective working relationships with other areas or individuals?
Address problem areas (arising from the above analysis)?

Reproduced from *Building a Better Team*,
by Peter Moxon, Gower, Aldershot, 1993.

Team purpose and goals

Purpose

- To help the group to identify its primary purpose.
- To gain commitment to the group's objectives.

Application

- This exercise can be used at any stage of group development to test individual assumptions about the team's role and their objectives. This is significant because it is those same assumptions that determine the personal behaviours of team members. Without a common focus and shared priorities it will be extremely difficult for any team to be effective.
- With a newly established group, it will force them to stand back and review what exactly is the role of their team. For a project team, this will mean revisiting and clarifying their brief and each team member's interpretation of it.
- For an ongoing team, it will make them differentiate between the team's common purpose versus that of each individual member (i.e. Why exactly do they need to exist as a team? What are their collective responsibilities?).
- With a long-standing team, it will allow them to test if the initial role they agreed is still valid or has changed.

Time required

Total time		4 hours
Part I	Syndicate working and discussion	1 hour 30 minutes
Part II	Pair working and discussion	2 hours and 30 minutes

Materials needed

- Flipcharts, pads and pens.
- Acetate paper and pens.

– Copies of Examples of Objectives (Document 12.1) – see Notes below for requirement.

Process

Part I

Split the team into two syndicates. Ask each to consider and discuss their answers to the following question:

'What is unique about this team that cannot be accomplished by the members individually?'

Have them conclude their discussions writing a statement on a flipchart that completes the following sentence:

'The primary purpose of the team is to . . .'

Allow each syndicate 40 minutes to prepare their statement. Then bring the syndicates together to share and agree a final statement for the team – one which *all* members agree to and one which would help others outside the group understand the team's unique role.

Part II

Split the group into buzz groups of 2 or 3 and have each group write down the main result areas for which the team is responsible (e.g. costs, quality, new product introduction, supplier agreements). Allow 10 minutes for this.

Have them call out their answers and write the results on a flipchart. Work with the group and get them to simplify the list to 5 or 6 main headings. (For examples see Document 12.1, 'Examples of Objectives', at the end of the section.)

Split the group into two or threes and allocate up to two of the main key result areas to each sub-group. Ask each sub-group to discuss their allocated areas and, using a time frame of the next 12 months, to prepare specific objectives for discussion and agreement with the group. They should test each objective to make sure that they are:

– Specific
– Measurable
– Achievable
– Realistic
– Timed

(See Document 12.1 for examples of good objectives.) Allow them up to 1 hour to work in their sub-groups and to write their proposed objectives on a flipchart.

Bring the group together and have each sub-group share and agree the objectives. It may be that some areas will need further investigation outside the session for specific targets to be included. If this is the case, have them agree an action plan detailing how they will finalize the objective.

Lastly, have the group agree the method by which they will review progress and modify objectives over time.

Notes

- If the group is not accustomed to working with objectives or is unskilled at writing specific, measurable targets, it may be necessary to provide a short training input with examples. A list of typical objectives, with measures to be taken, is given in Document 12.1.
- When allocating result areas to sub-groups, an alternative method is to allow each individual to decide which areas they work on. In this case ensure that sub-groups have no more than 3 team members, with each sub-group allocated at least two objective areas. (Whilst it is possible to work on each objective with the whole group it tends to be very laborious.)
- With groups who are unaccustomed to working with object-ives, it may take two sessions to finalize clear, agreed objectives. If this is the case, use the first session to shape the broad framework, and allocate pairs to work on the objectives before the second session. Start the second session with the pairs presenting back their work.
- Once the objectives have been finalized, it would be worth-while asking the group to consider if there are any persons or other groups that would benefit from knowing the objectives that they will be working to. If so, get the group to agree how they will share their objectives with those people.

Variation – for use with project teams

- With a 'project team' set-up that has an initial brief, have the leader summarize their brief and ask the syndicates to work on the following questions:

What fears, questions and concerns do you have regarding the brief?

What will success look like – 6 months hence, and 12 months hence?

What do you see as the primary role of the team in achieving the brief?

The purpose, when they present back and discuss the outcomes of their syndicate work, is to ensure they have a common understanding of the brief they have been given and have addressed any concerns and issues relating to it. Until these matters have been debated, it will be difficult to agree the team's primary objectives towards achieving the brief. Once agreement has been reached, however, the group can then progress to Part II, outlining specific objectives. Again, you may wish to consider splitting Parts I and II into two separate sessions or extending the session to a full day, depending on the circumstances.

Document 12.1

Examples of Objectives

Production

Reduce backorders from 36 per month average to 10 by year end.

Achieve rolling monthly average of 95% of approved schedule delivered (vs. 87% last year).

Costs

Reduce manufactured unit costs from last year's average of 80 per unit to 76 by year end.

Reduce wastage on lines 2 and 3 to 3% by . . .

Quality

No more than 3 product recalls to occur in 1992.

Completion of phase I implementation of Total Quality initiative by 31st October.

Capital installation

Develop and gain Board approval to Site Capital Budget by 30th April.

Completion of line upgrades for lines 6 and 7 by 30th September.

Subordinate development

Launch new appraisal programme by . . . and complete training of all staff by . . .

Develop succession plan for site, agreeing potential successors for top 20 managers by . . .

Sales

Increase product sales of Brand X by 200,000 by end of 3rd Quarter.

Launch Brand Y on 1st March meeting all pre-launch shipments and with no 'out-of stocks' for the first 6 months after launch.

Reproduced from *Building a Better Team*,
by Peter Moxon, Gower, Aldershot, 1993.

Decision-making process

This exercise is based on a technique called 'Responsibility Charting' in R. Beckhard and R. T. Harris (1987) *Organisational Transitions – Managing Complex Change*, OD series, Addison Wesley.

Purpose

- To clarify the decision-making processes and authority levels, either within a single group or between two teams.
- To identify areas of confusion or conflict and agree actions to resolve any issues.

Application

- This exercise can be run within an existing group to clarify the specific involvement of members with respect to the main decisions and activities of the group. It can be used to help to clarify the boundary between staff and line or the authority level between the team leader and the team.
- It is equally useful in clarifying the interface between two different teams (e.g. a specialist team and the line team they service).
- The structured approach helps reduce potential conflict caused by assumption and generalization.
- It will generally require the involvement of a facilitator who can concentrate on the process. This allows all the parties to participate fully in the discussion and will certainly assist in preventing the session from becoming swamped in detail.
- It is best to run the exercise as a single session, and it will take up to 8 hours to complete. When run with two teams, pre-briefing of each team and some pre-work is essential to ensure maximum discussion time during the session.

Time required

Total time

Up to 2 hours for pre-work and 8 hours for the team session

Part I	Pre-work	1–2 hours
Part II	Introduction	15 minutes
	Agreement of task list	30 minutes
Part III	Charting responsibilities	2–4 hours
Part IV	Summary of role	45 minutes
Part V	Action planning	1–2 hours

Materials needed

- Flipcharts and pens.
- Copies of completed pre-work for all participants.

Process

The process described below has been written for a situation where *two* different teams are clarifying the decision-making process between them. (If used with a *single* group, the same broad process is followed but can be much simplified and the overall time shortened. With a small group, pre-work assignments can be completed through syndicate work or as a group discussion *during* the working session.)

Part I

This part is carried out separately with each of the two teams.

A thorough pre-briefing is needed of both participating teams or, at the least, the two team leaders. At the briefing you will need to run through the aims of the exercise and the overall programme.

The process involves collating a list of the main activities in which the two groups are engaged, and having both groups systematically agree responsibilities, involvement levels and authority levels for each activity. Clarification and agreement is through joint discussion between the teams, which will identify problem areas for resolution. The outcome will be a fairly specific description of how the two teams interface. The process will also reveal problem areas that may require further work by both groups.

The pre-work for each group is to consider the specific areas in which the teams interface and are, to varying extents, inter-dependent. For each of the areas, the teams have to list the main

activities and key decisions that need to be taken. For example, if we consider a central engineering team and a production team in a factory, the areas of interdependence may include the following:

- Major project installation.
- Scheduled maintenance.
- Trouble-shooting problems.
- Minor projects, etc.

It is possible to break down each area into activities. For example, under 'major project installation' this could include the following:

- Defining the project scope.
- Deciding on contractors.
- Defining and deciding the final design.
- Purchase of new equipment.
- Install equipment.
- Agreement of completion and handover.

Clearly, any one of these activities is a potential source of confusion or conflict if both parties have differing expectations of who is responsible or who takes decisions.

A deadline should be set for the lists to be returned to you before the workshop. You should then collate them into a master list that can be tested with each team before the working session. The aim is to agree the list with both groups *before the session*. The list will then form the basis for discussion during the session.

At this stage, do not ask either group to think about who is responsible for what activity.

Part II

Open the joint session by repeating the objectives, and state that most of the day will be taken up with discussing, item by item, the lists previously prepared and collated, agreeing detailed responsibilities.

Tell the group that you will be asking them to consider each area's activities and to make decisions on the following points:

- Who is **responsible**   **(R)**
- Who carries the **authority**   **(A)**
- Who must provide **support**   **(S)**
- Who must be **informed**   **(I)**

Explain that on most activities they will probably reach quick agreement. Where they do not, you will want them to discuss the issues concerned, come to an agreement and make a decision. For most situations, this will be possible. Where agreement is not reached fairly quickly write the issues on a flipchart for further discussion later in the day.

Take the group through the definitions and the basic rules of allocating them.

Responsibility — Is charged with 'making it happen' – from the beginning to the end of the action. May not personally perform the action (e.g. may delegate it to one of his or her own subordinates) but is fully responsible. Only one person can be allocated an R.

Authority — Has the 'right of veto' and must approve before decision or action is taken. There should be as few As as possible – too many will reduce effectiveness.

Support — Is charged with providing support in the form of resources but has no 'right of veto'.

Inform — Needs to be informed or consulted before action is taken but again has no 'right of veto'. (This does *not* include those people who would be informed for information purposes after the event.)

Major project installation	Project Engineer	Production Manager	Plant Manager	Central Engineering Manager	Accounts Manager
1. Define project scope and cost	R	A	A		S
2. Decide contractors	A			R	
3. Agree final design and budget	R	A	A	S	I
4. Purchase new equipment	S			R	
5. Install equipment	R	S		S	
6. Agree completion and handover	R	A		A	

Figure 15: Example of responsibility chart

The allocation of the **R**s, **A**s, **S**s, **I**s for each activity will be to who may be within or outside the two groups. For example, in the 'purchase of new equipment' mentioned in the engineering illustration above the allocation may break down as follows:

- Responsibility   Project Engineering Manager
- Authority   Production Manager and Project
                        Engineering Manager and Plant Manager
- Support   Central Engineering Purchaser
- Informed   Accounts Manager

(The Accounts Manager and Plant Manager, whilst not present at the session, must be listed if they have a part to play.)

At this stage, post up the list of areas and associated activities completed in the pre-work. List them down the left-hand side of the flipchart as illustrated in Figure 15. Use a separate chart for each area. Check with the group that they are comfortable with the various lists of activities. Make any amendments necessary.

Part II

Once the two teams have agreed the task list, continue the joint session by having them now assign responsibilities against each task or decision.

Starting separately with each of the defined areas ask the group to call out the main 'actors' involved and list them across the tops of the columns (e.g. production manager, electrical manager). (You may need to add to or delete the 'actors' involved as you work through each activity.) Then ask the group, for each activity, to allocate a single **R** and appropriate **A**s, **S**s and **I**s. Your role at this stage is simply to control the discussion, resolve any differences and ensure the whole group is comfortable with the decisions written down. If a reasonably quick decision cannot be reached, list this point for further debate on a separate flipchart and move on.

Your aim is to allow proper debate whilst making sure the group makes progress. Needless to say, it can be a laborious but necessary process with many activities. However, it is usual that the two teams will have a common perspective on most of the activities with only 10–20 per cent requiring discussion. The group will need some help at the early stage to fully understand the definitions (see above) but will speed up as the process continues.

On some occasions it may be necessary to break down an activity further to reach agreement. For example, 'purchase of new equipment' may need to be broken down into the following:

- Agreeing basic specifications.
- Identifying alternative suppliers.
- Agreeing final supplier.

Do not worry if this is the case, as it is all helping to remove ambiguity and create clarity. The eventual decisions may well depend more on the trust and relationship between the parties than on job descriptions. An example of what a completed grid will look like is illustrated in Figure 15.

Part IV

At the end of Part III, which can take 2–4 hours, split the total group into their own original two teams. Using the material generated in Part III have them list on separate sheets all the activities for which they are responsible (i.e. their **R**s), all the activities for which they have authority (i.e. **A**s), etc. Ask them to review the picture emerging and check that they are comfortable with the overall outcome.

Part V

Reconvene the full group and then have each team present their defined roles to the other team for final clarification and agreement.

At this point, there will be common agreement on virtually all the areas of interdependence. There are likely, however, to be a few outstanding issues which were separately listed on flipcharts during Part III. In discussion, the group now have either to come to a decision on each remaining issue or agree an action plan to progress the issue outside the meeting. The latter course is probable if the situation is complex and requires further investigation, and possibly the involvement of others not present. Any actions agreed must be recorded and a member assigned to follow them through.

As a final part of the discussion, ask the group to agree on the following points:

- How they will write up the outcomes and distribute them for future reference.
- How they will communicate the outcomes to other parties affected – especially if they have agreed changes to current practices.
- How and when they will review progress in the future.

The last point is most important if they are to continue any progress gained from discussions during the sessions.

Notes

- Part III will need to be planned and broken down into 'mini sessions' depending on the number of areas and activities listed. For example, if four areas are to covered, plan each to take about 45 minutes with a break after the first two are completed. It is advisable not to allow the time to run on beyond one and a half hours without a break.
- It is also advisable to prepare the flipcharts for Part III before the joint working session, leaving spaces to allow for any changes or additions.

Allocation of R, A, S and I – points to consider

- When assigning the **R**s, **A**s etc, start with the responsibility (**R**) and ensure only *one* 'actor' is assigned this role. Then agree the allocation of **A, S** and **I**. If the group is struggling to allocate responsibility to one person, consider breaking the task down to sub-activities.
- Minimize the number of **A**s for any one action or decision. The more **A**s, the slower the decision. Have the group negotiate to change some **A**s to **S**s or **I**s.
- It is possible for the 'actor' responsible (**R**) also to carry the full authority (**A**). With this exception, in all other cases there should only be one letter per box on the grid.
- If the group simply cannot agree, suggest that they refer the situation higher up the organization for a decision.
- With staff and line teams, when they summarize the outcome of all the discussions, the staff team may be surprised to find that they have more **S**s than **A**s. This reflects the fact that the staff unit is servicing the line. The line, however, must understand that the **S**s mean *consultation before action or decision*. In a healthy situation, whilst the staff team may not have the right of veto (**A**), they will be able to influence strongly the decisions made by the line team so that they do not feel impotent. It is these very feelings of impotence that often cause staff groups to seek rights of veto in order to gain access to influencing line decisions. In a healthy situation where collaboration is the norm, exercising any 'right of veto' is very much the last option.
- With groups in the 'forming' and 'storming' stages of development, it is probable that there will be multiple **A**s resulting from uncertainty, mistrust or an initial dependency on the leader.

– As a group develops, the leader should be actively trans-
  ferring his or her **A**s to the group and replacing them with **S**s.

Why is it that they
never seem to
achieve much in
their meetings?

Meetings review

Purpose

- To review the effectiveness of the group's meetings and agree actions to address any problems.

Application

- This exercise can be used with any group, and at any stage of their development.
- It provides a structured way for the group to review the purpose and content of their various meetings and the processes within each meeting (e.g. participation, chairmanship) etc.
- In the early stage of a group's development, meetings present a cameo of the team's effectiveness. Many of the issues inhibiting team performance (e.g. hidden agendas, poor relationships, unclear goals) are revealed during the meetings.
- Having the group review their meeting structures and process is a good way of leading them into discussion on the more fundamental issues that need to be resolved.

Time required

Total time		2 hours approximately
Part I	Syndicate working	1 hour
Part II	Presentation and discussion	1 hour

Materials needed

- Flipchart, pads and pens.
- Syndicate Briefing Sheets (Documents 14.1 and 14.2).
- Copies of Example Meeting Schedule (Document 14.3).

Process

Part I

Introduce the exercise by explaining that meetings are an inherent part of working together as an effective team. They form a primary mechanism for both communication and decision making within the group. However, they can also provide a source of continual frustration by being poorly structured and run.

Explain that with every meeting the group are faced with a dilemma of balancing both business and individual needs. They must therefore review both the purpose and content of their meetings (e.g. Why do they have them? What is each for? What should be covered? Who should attend?) and the processes within each meeting (e.g. chairmanship, participation, preparation etc.).

Split the group into two syndicates. State that you want the first syndicate to focus on the structure of their meetings (e.g. how many, what purpose and content etc.) and the second on the processes and skills displayed during their meetings. Give the first syndicate Briefing Sheet I and the second syndicate Briefing Sheet II. Ask each syndicate to consider the problems as they see them, to prepare recommendations for any changes needed, and also to prepare a summary of their conclusions for presentation and agreement. Allow the syndicates 1 hour for discussion and preparation of their presentations (15 minutes maximum).

Part II

At the end of this period, bring the syndicates together and have each present their outcomes. Start with the 'purpose and content' syndicate. After each presentation, allow questions of clarification only and then facilitate an open discussion of each syndicate's recommendations, helping the group make decisions on changes they believe will improve the situation. Some points to consider during the discussion on the structure of their meetings would be the following:

- **Challenge and test their thinking about the number of meetings and the attendance**. Many groups, particularly at the early stage of development when trust levels are low, may want all members to attend all meetings.
- **They should not try to satisfy all their needs in a single meeting**. This will result in highly varied participation, lengthy and ineffective meetings and individual frustrations.
- **Encourage them to think of meeting in sub-groups where**

177

necessary and to use other mechanisms to keep the rest of the group informed. Ensure that they consider the real need for each person's attendance. It can be far more effective for a team to hold 2–3 different meetings, with different purposes and different team members attending.

- **Challenge their reason for any regular meetings lasting beyond 2 hours.** Concentration and effectiveness will fall rapidly beyond this time. It may be necessary for them to hold a long meeting, however, on an infrequent basis, to be used more as a working session (e.g. to develop a particular strategy). If this is the case, question how they will plan to structure the meeting and ensure its effectiveness.
- **Make them think through how they will separate straight-forward information exchange with lengthier discussion and decision making.** It may be more productive to satisfy such needs separately. The former could be handled by an informal get-together each day, the latter by a planned fortnightly meeting.
- **Encourage them to take off the agenda for full group meetings any issues that only affect a small minority of members.** These issues will be better handled by those sub-groups meeting separately, and perhaps reporting back any conclusions reached to one of the group's information exchange meetings.
- **Ask the group to summarize and write on a flipchart the agreements they have reached.** Whatever the outcome of the discussion, it will be a compromise of some form but should result in better use of the group's and individual members' time. (An example meetings schedule is included at the end of this section as Document 14.3.)
- **As a final point, have them agree how and when they will review the working of their new structure.**

During the discussion on meeting processes, issues that may arise and need attention could be as follows:

- Unclear agendas – single topic headings that do not make clear why the agenda item is present and what outcomes are expected.
- Individual rather than group issues being raised at full team meetings.
- Over-presentation and repetition or lack of preparation by individuals.
- Clear action plans not agreed – what, who, by when – or actions not followed through and reviewed.

- Discussion not staying on track – tackling several issues at once.
- Variable participation and no clear chairmanship.
- Agendas too ambitious – time not allocated for each item or items allowed to overrun.

(A fuller description of discussions, and the problems associated with them, is outlined in Part II, pp. 62.) As with the first part of the discussion, ensure the group writes on a flipchart a summary of the decisions they have reached, for typing and distribution after the session.

From the discussions, ask the group to produce a list of meeting ground rules. If possible, encourage them to plan into each of their future meetings a 10-minute review at the end against their checklist of ground rules. In this way, they will increase their own self-awareness of behaviours and actions that are reducing the team's effectiveness in meetings.

Note

- One outcome of the second part of the discussion on the meeting process could well be the need for skills training on handling and running meetings. You will need to decide before the session the extent to which you want to move into this area during the session itself. The session could easily be combined with skills development on discussion leadership or meeting behaviours, using films and videoed exercises.

Document 14.1

Briefing Sheet I

The aim of this exercise is to review the effectiveness of team meetings and agree changes needed. Your syndicate is to concentrate on the structure of meetings needed by the team.

Discuss how you see the current structure of team meetings with regard to the following factors:

- The purpose and content of each meeting.
- The attendance at each meeting.
- The frequency and length of the meeting.

Review how the current meeting structure is fulfilling both the business needs and the needs of individuals within the team.

Consider any changes you feel are necessary and prepare a short presentation (15 minutes maximum), outlining any future structure proposed.

For each meeting planned clearly state its purpose, content, the minimum attendance necessary and the meeting's frequency and length.

Reproduced from *Building a Better Team*,
by Peter Moxon, Gower, Aldershot, 1993.

Briefing Sheet II

The aim of this exercise is to review the effectiveness of the team meetings and agree changes needed.

Your syndicate is to consider the effectiveness of previous meetings in the following areas and make recommendations to improve effectiveness in these areas:

- Preparation and organization.
- Participation.
- Chairmanship.
- Handling of conflicts or differences.
- Action planning and follow-up.

Prepare a short presentation (15 minutes maximum) outlining your conclusions for discussion and agreement with the other group.

Reproduced from *Building a Better Team*, by Peter Moxon, Gower, Aldershot, 1993.

Document 14.3 | Example Meeting Schedule

The schedule below illustrates the outcomes from a senior management team within a factory.

Meetings	Purpose	Attendance	Time/Venue
Factory manager's meeting	Information exchange (no formal agenda).	Voluntary	20 min. Daily 10am Room Y
Quarterly review	Weeks 1–3: Information exchange Varied agenda; discussion and agreement on short-term issues Week 4: – Monthly review of factory performance (45 min) – Presentations from other areas (e.g. marketing) (1hr) – Information exchange (15min) (formal agenda; items to Factory Manager by Monday p.m. External speakers allocated slot by Factory Manager)	All	2 hrs Weekly Thursday 11am Room Y
Quarterly review	– Review of quarterly performance (formal presentations – 2 hrs) – Discussion on strategic issues, or specific projects – single subject (agenda agreed and planned beforehand – 4hrs max.)	All	4 hrs Quarterly 1st Monday of month Room Y
Production meeting	Discussion/decisions on short-term production issues	Production Managers and Materials Manager	30 min. Tuesday, Thursday Room Z
Ad hoc meetings	Discussion/decisions on specific major issues that cannot wait for quarterly meeting	Dependent on topics	2 hrs max. As and when

Reproduced from *Building a Better Team*, by Peter Moxon, Gower, Aldershot, 1993.

Index

183

184

185

Problem Solving in Groups
Second Edition
Mike Robson

Modern scientific research has demonstrated that groups are likely to solve problems more effectively than individuals. As most of us knew already, two heads (or more) are better than one. In organizations it makes sense to harness the power of the group both to deal with problems already identified and to generate ideas for enhancing effectiveness by reducing costs, increasing productivity and the like.

In this revised and updated edition of his successful book, Mike Robson first introduces the concepts and methods involved. Then, after setting out the advantages of the group approach, he examines in detail each of the eight key problem solving techniques. The final part of the book explains how to present proposed solutions, how to evaluate results and how to ensure that the group process runs smoothly.

With its practical tone, its down-to-earth style and lively visuals, this is a book that will appeal strongly to managers and trainers looking for ways of improving their organization's and their department's performance.

Contents
Part I: Introduction • The benefits of group problem solving • Problem-solving groups • Part II: Problem-Solving Techniques • The problem-solving process • Brainstorming • Defining problems clearly • Analysing problems • Collecting data • Interpreting data • Finding solutions • Cost-benefit analysis • Part III: Following Through • Presenting solutions • Working together • Dealing with problems in the group • Index.

1993   178 pages   0 566 07414 1 Hardback   0 566 07415 X Paperback

Gower

How Managers Can Develop Managers

Alan Mumford

Managers are constantly being told that they are responsible for developing other managers. This challenging book explains why and how this should be done.

Moving beyond the familiar territory of appraisal, coaching and courses, Professor Mumford examines ways of using day-to-day contact to develop managers. The emphasis is on learning from experience - from the job itself, from problems and opportunities, from bosses, mentors and colleagues.

Among the topics covered are:
- recognizing learning opportunities
- understanding the learning process
- what being helped involves
- the skills required to develop others
- the idea of reciprocity ("I help you, you help me")

Throughout the text there are exercises designed to connect the reader's own experience to the author's ideas. The result is a powerful and innovative work from one of Europe's foremost writers on management development.

Contents

1993   200 pages   0 566 07403 6

Gower